FIELD GUIDE TO THE BIRDS OF BRITAIN AND IRELAND

Bloomsbury Natural History
An imprint of Bloomsbury Publishing Plc

50 Bedford Square
London
WC1B 3DP
UK

1385 Broadway
New York
NY 10018
USA

www.bloomsbury.com

First published 2016

A catalogue record for this book is available from the British Library.

Library of Congress Cataloguing-in-Publication data has been applied for.

ISBN: PB: 978-1-4729-1746-1

2 4 6 8 10 9 7 5 3 1

Design by Rod Teasdale

Printed and bound in China by C&C Offset Printing Co., Ltd.

FIELD GUIDE TO THE BIRDS OF BRITAIN AND IRELAND

Mark Golley

BLOOMSBURY
LONDON • NEW DELHI • NEW YORK • SYDNEY

CONTENTS

The Wildlife Trusts are the UK's largest people-powered organisation caring for all nature - rivers, bogs, meadows, forests, seas and much more. We are 47 Wildlife Trusts covering the whole of the UK with a shared mission to restore nature everywhere we can and to inspire people to value and take action for nature for future generations.

Together we care for thousands of wild places that are great for both people and wildlife. These include more than 760 woodlands, 500 grasslands and even 11 wildlife gardens. You're never too far away from your nearest Wildlife Trust nature reserve, and on average in England, you're only three miles away from escaping to the sounds and sights of nature that we protect.

Our goal is nature's recovery – on land and at sea. To achieve this we rely on the vital support of more than 800,000 members, 43,000 volunteers, donors, corporate supporters and funders. To find the Wildlife Trust that means most to you and lend your support, visit wildlifetrusts.org/your-local-trust

Importantly, we encourage people to experience wildlife for themselves. We believe that a deeper appreciation and connection to nature can start with a book such as this one by Mark Golley. We need more people to understand and value the birds and other wildlife that share our countryside with us.

Few realise just how endangered much of our British wildlife is. In recent years, once-common bird species such as the sparrow and starling have largely declined, mainly due to the demands that modern human-living has placed on habitats.

The Wildlife Trusts believe, however, that plenty can still be done to reverse the losses of the past, and that we all have a role to play in making this happen. One way to begin is by contacting your local Wildlife Trust for information on wildlife events, volunteering opportunities and the wild places that are close to you. Help us to protect wildlife for the future and become a member today. Visit www.wildlifetrusts.org for further information.

We hope that, with the help of this book, you have fun learning more about our British Birds and end up appreciating them just as much as we do!

The Wildlife Trusts is a registered charity (number 207238).

INTRODUCTION

In an introduction, it is always so hard to explain to the bookshop browser, the catalogue connoisseur or the 'stocking filler' shopper just what makes one bird book more appealing than one of the plethora of similar titles that adorn the shelves.

The first question that needs to be asked is 'who is *Field Guide to the Birds of Britain and Ireland* aimed at?'

Well, this is a book both for the beginner and also the novice, as well as those with a little more birdwatching experience too. Primarily, it is a book for those with a passion for birds.

Next we need to ascertain what distinguishes this title from the abundance of related titles on the shelf. What makes one book 'better' than another that seems so similar? Much of it is to do with price, personal preference, layout, readability of the text, and above all else, the quality and warmth found amongst the mass of illustrations. If all these meet the buyer's own criterion, then there is one final factor that may be decisive and that is just how easy to use the book is, whether checking notes made in the field or when you get back to the car or the house.

Some find the systematic lists of the heftier field guides a little confusing as you forever thumb up and down searching for a certain species. It could also be said that for many more casual birdwatchers, the bigger field guides can be a little overwhelming in the number of species which are often irrelevant (and possibly even confusing) in a purely British and Irish birdwatching context.

This guide does have some systematic points to deal with – hopefully conveyed in a user-friendly way - but the species chosen are ones that you will see (with the all important luck and perseverance) in the glorious variety of habitats that make up Britain and Ireland. The descriptions are written in a straightforward manner and are sound companions for the delightful illustrations. Hopefully then, you will take a peek at *this* particular book and think that is made for you.

How this book works

The aim of the book is to be an easy, informed read with a wealth of illustrations to help you with most of the identification challenges that you may come across whilst birdwatching in this country. There are over 280 species described and illustrated here, and the primary aim is for user-friendly text and artwork to guide you towards conclusive identification remedies. Wherever you may live, wherever you may head away to for your birdwatching, the spread of species here covers a broad range of our different resident and visiting birds found amongst a wide range of familiar habitats too.

What else do you get on the page? As well as super artwork, there are measurements (taken from bill tip to tail tip of a live bird); a brief introductory paragraph on the species; notes on where and when to find the species; possible confusion species and also short, bite-sized paragraphs full of identification tips. Finally, there are notes on the all-important calls too.

This book does follow recognized taxonomy and nomenclature, using the *List of Recent Holarctic Bird Species* (Voous, 1977) as the standard. This is widely used in many publications but, as with other recent guides, this book has also incorporated more recent work on taxonomy and nomenclature, most notably *Palearctic Birds* (Beaman, 1994).

The taxonomy of birds is a subject that creates untold chat and discussion worldwide and for the beginner and the novice, there's no reason to embed yourself with the chop and change of science. One much more important aspect of birdwatching, though not nearly as laborious as avian taxonomics, is topography. Even a basic grasp of the correct terminology of what's where on a bird will help you improve your birdwatching skills (and your enjoyment) no end. What's more, it's becomes great fun as you see things fall into place whilst out and about in the field - no more confusion over what's an eyestripe and what's a supercilium when you scribble a few notes on something in front of you!

The parts of a bird

Most of this book avoids overly complex topographical detail, but it does appear occasionally - knowing the difference between the median and greater coverts or the secondaries from the primaries may make all the difference. But don't be daunted by it - the terms *will* fall into place and you may enjoy your birdwatching all the more if you become familiar with at least some of the main terms.

As well as learning the more difficult things such as the names of feather tracts, there are a number of things that you can do to improve your identification technique.

Always try to judge the size of the bird by comparing it to either another species close to it or even by objects nearby, be it a tin can, a brick, or even a leaf.

Take note of the shape, as well as the size of the bird. Remember though that weather may change the shape of a bird - looking sleek in hot weather, or puffed up in cold conditions.

Remember to try and note exactly the colours on the bird and where they are.

Listen to any calls or song the bird gives - it's fiendishly hard to transcribe them, but try to commit familiar species to memory first and, in time, others will follow.

See if the bird has any particular behavioural traits and always be aware of exactly what sort of habitat it's in.

Think about the time of year... you are unlikely to see a Waxwing in July or a Cuckoo in January!

Finally, make sure you have a few basic essentials with you - binoculars (use what you feel comfortable with and what you can afford); a good quality lens cloth (there's no point paying upwards of £1800 for a pair of 'bins' only to clean away the coatings with a grotty tissue!); a notebook and pencil (a 'police style' one is perfect) and *Field Guide to the Birds of Britain and Ireland,* too! Most importantly, always take your enthusiasm along with you - with that, you can't fail.

Good birding!

Mark Golley

Redwing

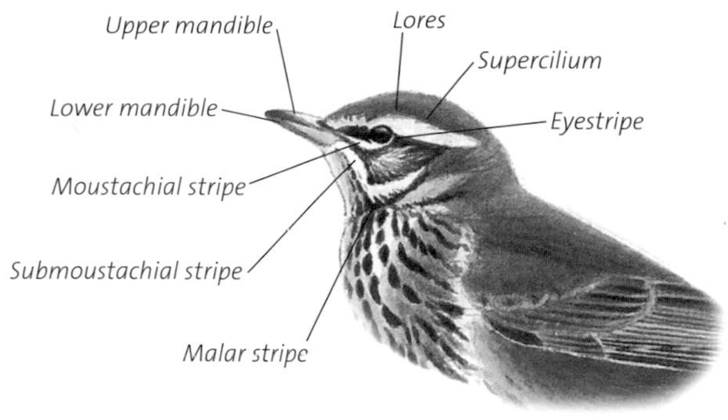

Cuckoo

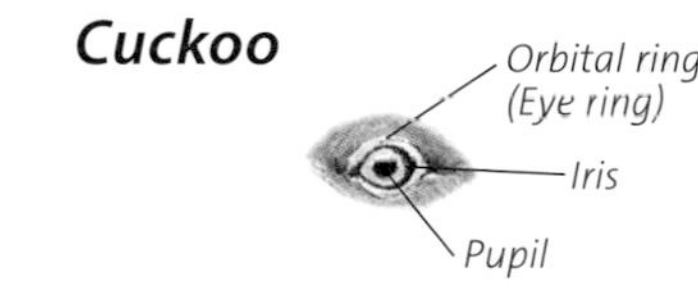

Female Reed Bunting

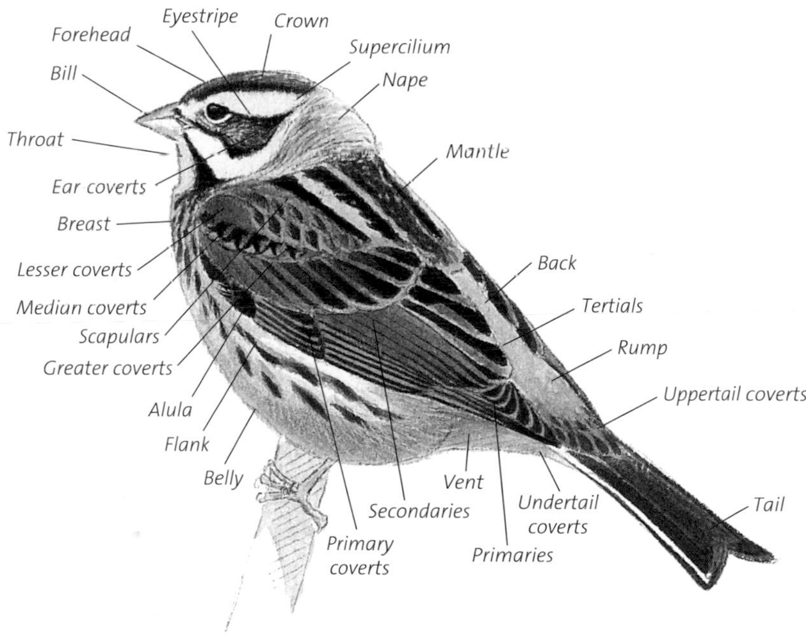

HABITATS

Coastal birds

Coastal habitats include cliffs, dunes and beaches, woods and scrub, fields and hedgerows, estuaries and rivers. One of the many joys of such varied areas within one habitat is that there is always something to see and somewhere to go at any time of year, and at any time of day. As with all the other habitats dealt with, spring and summer offer most birding opportunities, if only in terms of the hours of daylight in which to go birding in. Unlike other habitats, however, coastal sites are equally as good, some would say better, in the autumn and winter months.

When birding coastal sites it can be difficult to know what optics to take. A telescope is recommended, whether searching through hundreds of waders at a winter roost or summer flocks of terns. However, a telescope is essential for seawatching, especially in autumn.

Seawatching isn't to everyone's liking - the thought of sitting on a beach exposed to the wind and rain really is pretty off-putting, but the sight of skuas, shearwaters, petrels, Gannets and Fulmars careering across the waves makes it all worthwhile.

Wetland birds

As you will notice, there are many variations on the Wetland theme, but most can be watched in a similar way. Whether you are at a reservoir, a marshy lagoon or alongside some of our larger rivers, you may find that a pair of binoculars aren't quite enough for you. If that's the case, you may need to think about using a telescope. Although initially cumbersome, birding wetlands becomes far more pleasurable with one. Many wetland sites boast hides for you to watch from, and footpaths that you can wander around, all without disturbing the birds. The optimum periods for heading to wetland sites is seasonally dependant: spring and autumn are particularly good, even at sites which are many miles from the coast. They are frequently used as stop-off points by waders or terns moving across the country, navigating by using major river courses and estuaries. Many birdwatchers feel that reservoirs, marshes and rivers come into their own during winter months, when wildfowl and gulls join the throng. If you regularly visit a wetland, you'll soon begin to pick up on the best times and conditions to visit. Autumn can be a wonderful time as migrants hustle and bustle for food as they prepare for a southbound passage, or as new arrivals replenish themselves after arriving from their own distant summer breeding grounds.

Woodland birds

Birding a good area of woodland can be one of the most rewarding aspects of bird-watching almost anywhere in Britain and Ireland. More often than not, you can leave the heavy 'scope and tripod at home and just use your binoculars.

Few would argue with the fact that a boisterous spring dawn chorus is one of the most thrilling events in the ornithological calendar and almost any woodland can provide a variety of species. If you feel a little unsure about trying to identify all the bird song on your own, how about heading out on a guided dawn chorus event? There are many county wildlife trusts and bird conservation groups that run events like this during the spring.

You can visit woods at any time of the day and at any time of the year (winter is often the quietest season in a wood) and there will almost always be birds to see. Although there may be fewer numbers of birds in winter, they are much easier to spot and therefore identify due to the lack of dense foliage. Early and late visits are often best; birds get a little sleepy in the middle of the day. Always be as quiet as you can, so that you can pick up the more subtle calls. Standing in one spot for a while is a good idea. If it seems quiet, move on. Different types of woodland will host different types of birds. Some species overlap between deciduous and coniferous woods, but some woodland is very specialized, such as the Caledonian forests of Scotland.

Farmland birds

Farmland habitats are, at first glance, some of the less appealing areas to visit, especially in this age of mono-cultures and hedgerow-free zones. Thankfully, this sad scene is limited to areas of southern England, elsewhere, there are some beautiful areas of bird–rich farmland, home to a diverse range of species, some of which are pretty scarce. Many of the species seen on farmland are resident and seen at anytime of the year (crows, partridges and Pheasant), but some (Stone Curlew, Quail and wild geese) are seasonally dependant. You may need to visit throughout the year, and often visit different areas of farmland across the country to see some species - it will always be worth it when a Montagu's Harrier drifts over an East Anglian barley field, or a Corncrake rasps away from a Hebridean iris bed. Often the telescope can stay at home when searching farmland areas for most species, but it is essential when scanning distant geese flocks. Species such as Pink-footed Goose are prone to disturbance on their wintering grounds, be it deliberate or inadvertent. Far better to view them from a distance, revelling in the sights and sounds as they go about their daily routine.

Urban birds

Birding within a large town or city may seem rather unrewarding, from both an aesthetic point of view and with regard to the number of species you may see. This may be true to an extent, but, as with birding in any other area of the country, you get as much out as you put into it.

Imagine the pleasure of seeing a flock of migrant thrushes flying over a city centre in the first days of autumn, or seeing a Grey Wagtail flit along wet guttering in winter, as all around you seem immune to the outside world. It doesn't even have to be the unexpected that brings enjoyment to the urban birdwatcher - the sight of Feral Pigeons being 'spooked' by a passing Kestrel, or vast numbers of roosting Pied Wagtails in a city centre, all add to the diversity of an often neglected habitat.

Of course, it is not just buildings that make up the urban birdwatching habitat - there are open areas of green in most towns, be it parkland or a small garden. You may feel a little self-conscious wandering along with a pair of binoculars, but it doesn't last! And when you spy the first returning Swift of the year, see a roosting Tawny Owl, or hear the scratchy warble of a male Black Redstart, you'll be oblivious to everything else.

Urban birdwatching has also benefited conservationists - the decline of the House Sparrow in the mid 90s first became apparent when birdwatchers started to ask 'Where have they all gone?' Along with the importance of urban breeding species like Peregrine, the worth of cities and towns as bird habitats should not be underestimated.

Upland birds

Another specialised habitat and perhaps one of the hardest areas in which to go birding, if only because of all the hills! Many of the species found in upland habitats are sedentary and can be seen at almost any time of year. Others are migratory and arrive from April to May, departing in early autumn. Many species can be seen at almost any time of the day, although Golden and White-tailed Eagles will wait for some degree of warmth before taking to the air. A pre-dawn trip to look for lekking Black Grouse is also well worth the

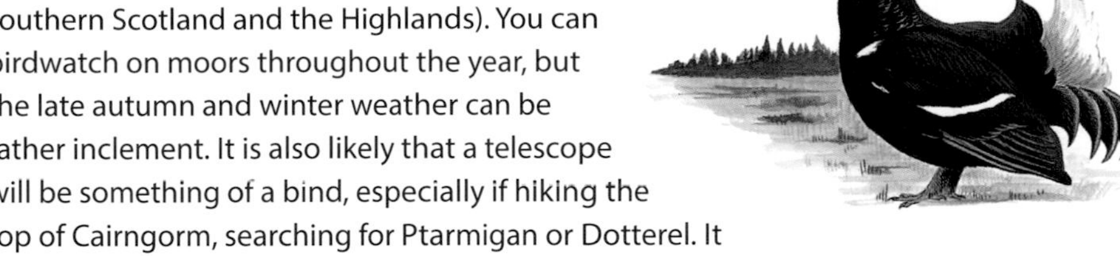

effort, if you are in the right part of the country (nowadays, the moors of north-east England, southern Scotland and the Highlands). You can birdwatch on moors throughout the year, but the late autumn and winter weather can be rather inclement. It is also likely that a telescope will be something of a bind, especially if hiking the top of Cairngorm, searching for Ptarmigan or Dotterel. It is vital to take note of your surroundings when in upland areas; an Ordnance Survey map is recommended and a compass is also very useful. Safety is paramount when birdwatching in upland areas, particularly in the Scottish mountains. The weather can turn pretty quickly on the tops, even during the summer. Always ensure that you are properly prepared for your day on the hills - pop waterproofs, a thermos and food in a rucksack, along with that map and compass.

Heathland birds

Heathlands are perhaps one of the most specialised areas of habitat that you will visit on a birdwatching outing. Although they have less bird species, they are still fabulous areas to visit. The species you do find on heathland areas are some of the most enigmatic you will encounter anywhere.

As with many other habitats, heathland birdwatching is often best in the early morning, particularly in the spring and summer. However, this is not always the case. Some species, such as Stonechat and the delightful Dartford Warbler, can be seen at any time of day and at any time of the year. Others, though, are migrants only, such as the ever-increasing Hobby. If the habitat is suitable, the weather warm and you have time to spare on a summer night, you could see and hear a Nightjar.

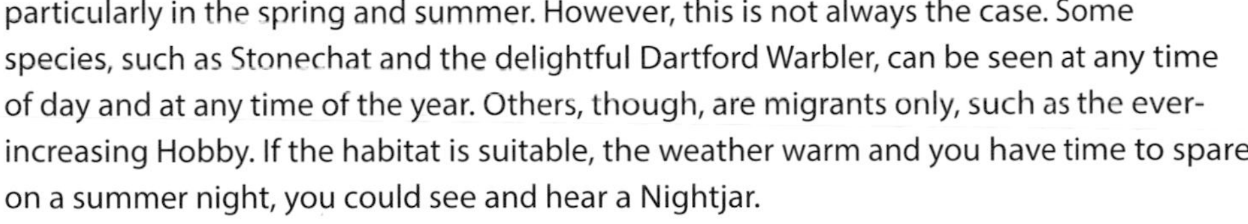

You may benefit from taking a telescope on heathland, although it is not essential, as many species tend to be fairly approachable. In the autumn and winter, head to higher ground and scan the trees and bushes for raptors (Merlin and Hen Harrier use heathlands as feeding and, sometimes, roost sites). If you are very lucky and in the right place, you may even find a Great Grey Shrike.

Due to the delicate nature of our heathland, a little caution is always advised. Try to stick to paths through the heather, rather than forge ahead on your own. Some of the species nesting in and around our heaths are Schedule One status, so disturbing them is actually an offence.

Mute Swan • *Cygnus olor*

140–160cm, 55–63in

When Throughout the year **Where** Freshwater and estuaries. Often in parks, lakes and also marshes **Confusion species** Bewick's and Whooper Swan, Spoonbill (in flight only) **Call** Mainly heard in spring, a rasping *herr-ahh*

▲In flight, **Mute Swans** (left) look largest, orange bills obvious, even at long range. Their wings whistle in flight. **Whoopers** (middle) are longer-necked and larger-bodied than **Bewick's** (right). You may also be able to see the different bill patterning at closer range.

▼One of the most familiar birds to be seen in Britain and Ireland. Large, white birds with distinctive bills. **Adults** are easy to identify. Wholly white plumage contrasts with their bill, orange with a black tip and large, black knob on the forehead, also black lores.

▼**Juveniles** are a subdued, greyer version of the adult. Upperparts are washed grey-brown. The youngster's bill is dull pink, with a less-glossy tip and knob.

Bewick's Swan • *Cygnus columbianus*

115–127cm, 45–49in

When Arrives from late autumn, staying into early spring **Where** Found on grazing meadows, damp pasture, farmland, mainly southern Britain **Confusion species** Whooper Swan **Call** Goose-like honking, higher-pitched than Whooper

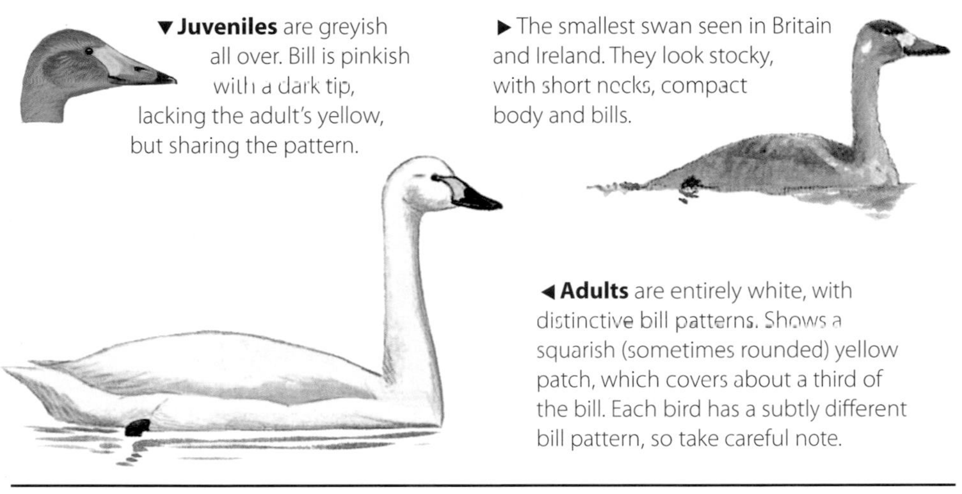

▼**Juveniles** are greyish all over. Bill is pinkish with a dark tip, lacking the adult's yellow, but sharing the pattern.

▶ The smallest swan seen in Britain and Ireland. They look stocky, with short necks, compact body and bills.

◀ **Adults** are entirely white, with distinctive bill patterns. Shows a squarish (sometimes rounded) yellow patch, which covers about a third of the bill. Each bird has a subtly different bill pattern, so take careful note.

Whooper Swan • *Cygnus cygnus*

140–160cm, 55–63in

When Arrives in late autumn **Where** Similar habitats to Bewick's Swan. More common in northern Britain and Ireland **Confusion species** Bewick's and Mute Swan **Call** Loud *whoop-whoop*, especially noisy in flight

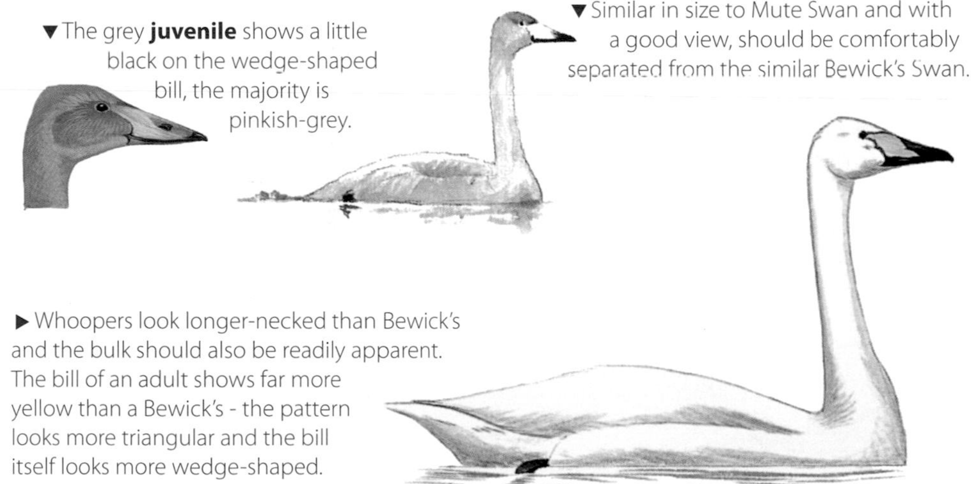

▼ The grey **juvenile** shows a little black on the wedge-shaped bill, the majority is pinkish-grey.

▼ Similar in size to Mute Swan and with a good view, should be comfortably separated from the similar Bewick's Swan.

▶ Whoopers look longer-necked than Bewick's and the bulk should also be readily apparent. The bill of an adult shows far more yellow than a Bewick's - the pattern looks more triangular and the bill itself looks more wedge-shaped.

Taiga/Tundra Bean Goose • *Anser fabalis* 69-88cm, 33in

When Arrives late October/early November. Stays into early spring **Where** Arable grazing fields, inland or coastal. Taigas in southern Scotland and east Norfolk. Tundras mainly in eastern Britain **Confusion species** Pink-footed Goose **Call** Deep, nasal *angk-angk*

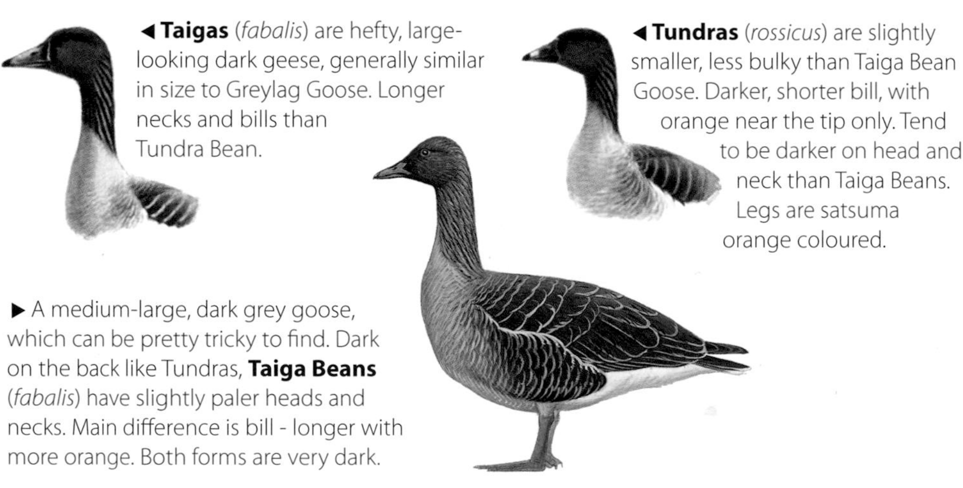

◀ **Taigas** (*fabalis*) are hefty, large-looking dark geese, generally similar in size to Greylag Goose. Longer necks and bills than Tundra Bean.

◀ **Tundras** (*rossicus*) are slightly smaller, less bulky than Taiga Bean Goose. Darker, shorter bill, with orange near the tip only. Tend to be darker on head and neck than Taiga Beans. Legs are satsuma orange coloured.

▶ A medium-large, dark grey goose, which can be pretty tricky to find. Dark on the back like Tundras, **Taiga Beans** (*fabalis*) have slightly paler heads and necks. Main difference is bill - longer with more orange. Both forms are very dark.

Pink-footed Goose • *Anser brachyrhynchus* 64-76cm, 28in

When Appears from September, leaves by early-mid April **Where** Coastal farmland, notably in eastern Scotland, Norfolk and Lancashire **Confusion species** Taiga/Tundra Bean Goose, White-fronted Goose **Call** In flight, high-pitched *wink-wink* or ringing, far-carrying *ung-ung-unk*

▼ A small, compact, attractive grey goose. Round-headed, with small bills and distinctive plumage. Often fly in V formation.

Close relative of the Bean Geese (not so long ago they were thought to be the same species).

▼ Dark brown head, contrasting with the greyish-looking wings (often looking scaly due to paler tips) and buff-brown chest and flanks, and white rear belly and undertail. Dark bill tip with pinkish base. Pink legs and feet.

White-fronted Goose • *Anser albifrons*

64-78cm, 29in

When From late October onwards, leaves in early spring **Where** Traditional wintering sites, in Ireland, Scotland and southern England **Confusion species** Pink-footed Goose **Call** An excited, high-pitched *kyu-you-you*

Medium-sized geese, compact, with shortish neck. Wintering birds arrive from two different- looking populations, Russia and Greenland.

▲ **White-fronted Goose** (left) **Pink-footed** (centre) **Greylag** (right).

▶ **Juveniles** lack white blaze on forehead, and the heavy black barring of adult. Separable from European juveniles by size, plumage and bill colour.

▶ **European White-fronted Goose** (*albifrons*).

▶ **Adult Greenlands** (*flavirostris*) winter in Ireland, Scotland, East Anglia. Adults are told from Russian adults by the longish, heavier orange bill, overall darker plumage, almost wholly dark tail. Appear slightly larger and chunkier.

Greylag Goose • *Anser anser*

74–84cm, 32in

When Feral birds throughout the year, breeding birds similar **Where** Genuine Greylags breed in Western Isles, some in Ireland. Feral birds on park lakes, ponds **Confusion species** Other grey geese **Call** Honking, noisy call - flocks can be very vocal

Found commonly in many areas of Britain, and is a large, rather plain-looking bird.

▶ Undertail is white. The bill is orange, legs dull-pinkish.

▶ Bulky birds, generally fawn-grey all over, slightly paler on the underparts, with a trace of some barring on the belly.

Canada Goose • *Branta canadensis*

90-100cm, 36-39in

When Throughout the year. Wild birds in winter only **Where** Feral birds on park lakes, rivers and marshes. Genuine vagrants on farmland and estuaries, often in Ireland and Scotland **Confusion species** None **Call** Loud, di-syllabic honking

◀ An extremely common sight across the whole of Britain and Ireland. Originally introduced from North America, the Canada Goose is now established firmly as one of our best-known waterbirds.

Interestingly, several of the smaller, darker forms of Canada Goose have turned up in parts of Britain and Ireland as wild vagrants.

▶ Large birds with long necks and contrasting plumage. Head and neck are black, except for a white patch on side of face. Underparts are buff- white and upperparts are grey-brown, with a white rump and black tail. Black bill, eye and legs.

Barnacle Goose • *Branta leucopsis*

58-70cm, 26in

When Begin to arrive from September onwards. Leave in late winter **Where** Coastal farmland in Scotland and Ireland. Feral flocks in southern England **Confusion species** Canada Goose **Call** An almost dog-like barking *kaw*

◀ In flight, shows more white on its face and looks smaller than Canada Goose.

A medium-sized goose, fairly compact with thick, short neck, smallish round head and small bill.

◀ The creamy face patch contrasts with the black head and neck. The upperparts are steely- grey with intricate black and white edges to the feathers. Rump is white and the tail black. Underparts silvery white. Eyes are black, greyish legs, small black bill.

Brent Goose • *Branta bernicla*

55-62cm, 24in

When Begin to arrive from early September onwards, leaving in spring. A few summer on east coast **Where** Coastal marshes and grazing meadows in southern England, East Anglia and Ireland **Confusion species** None **Call** A low-pitched, growling *krronc*

◀ In flight, Brent Geese form large, tightly-packed flocks. Preferring to fly fast and low, they make a familiar sight over saltmarshes and fields. Large flocks can be seen in winter as they arrive from northern Europe.

▲ ▶ There are two distinct forms of Brent Goose commonly seen. Both small, dark geese with small bills. **Juveniles** of both forms lack the white neck patches, appearing by first winter. Wings have pale bars.

▶ **Dark-bellied Brent Goose** (*bernicla*) (back) is a small goose with a black head and neck, with a white slash. The patterning on the underparts is variable, with plenty of pale mixing into the grey. The rear end is white. The upperparts are dark charcoal, with darker-looking wings. The tail is white with black outer feathers.

▶ **Pale-bellied form**(*hrota*) (front) is structurally almost identical to the Dark-bellied, perhaps slightly more pot-bellied. Note the colour of the underparts – the breast and belly are off-white with greyer smears, completely different to Dark-bellied Brent.

Snow Goose • *Anser caerulescens*

65-75cm, 27in

When In winter, some early spring records **Where** Grazing areas shared with other geese, by coasts, marshes or arable fields. Mainly in northern England, Scotland and Ireland **Confusion species** None **Call** Rarely heard amongst the noise of other species

▼ Approximately the same size as a Pink-footed Goose. They are entirely white, except for black wingtips.The triangular bill is pink, with a black 'grinning' patch

▲ Rather a small member of the group, but unmistakable if seen. A dark colour form (Blue Snow Goose) sometimes appears, but beware of hybrids.

Egyptian Goose • *Alopochen aegyptiacus*

63-73cm, 25-28in

When Throughout the year. Large flocks in autumn **Where** Large feral population in East Anglia, also southern England in smaller numbers. Ornamental lakes as well as marshes and rivers **Confusion species** Ruddy Shelduck (in flight only) **Call** Dry, rasping *haarunk*.

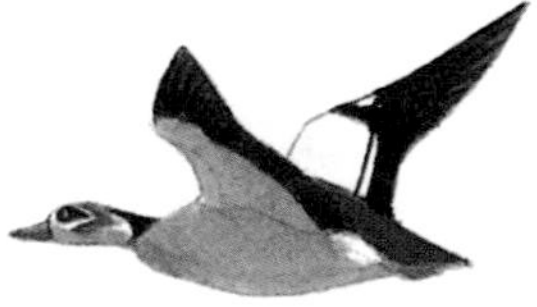

◀ In flight, shows an obvious, large, white wing panel, black, dark bottle- green and rufous primaries and trailing edge of the wing. The dark eye patch surround is easily seen.

A curious-looking bird, introduced to Britain from Africa during the 18th century. Larger than both Common and Ruddy Shelducks.

▶ Mainly dark, sandy- brown above and a dull- buff below. Rather ugly- looking face, off-white or grey with dark eye patch. Pink legs rather than the black of Ruddy Shelduck.

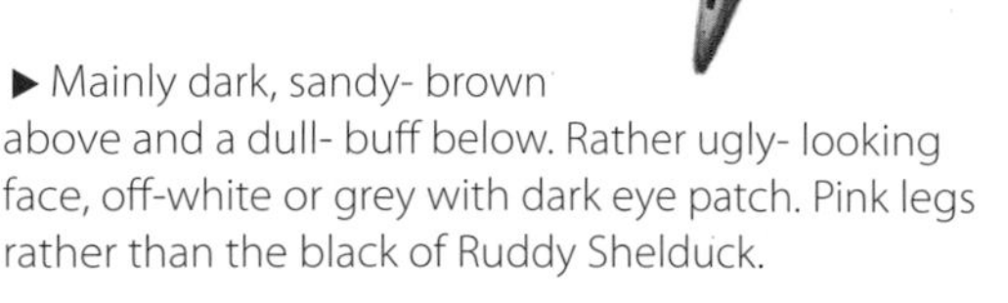

Shelduck • *Tadorna todorna*

55-65cm, 25in

When Throughout the year **Where** Mainly coastal, also inland near gravel pits and reservoirs **Confusion species** Egyptian Goose, Ruddy Shelduck **Call** A lovely whistle, interspersed with the odd grunt or two.

A fairly unmistakable, large, plump duck with a demeanour more in keeping with a goose. They are burrow-nesting birds, but have been known to hatch youngsters in tree holes or under buildings.

▲ In flight, the dark head and red bill are obvious.The black and white wings are rather long and pointed. Often whistles in flight.

▼ **Juveniles** (left) look vaguely comical once full-grown. Head and mantle are mottled dark grey and white. Overall, the plumage tones are much more subdued than the adults; bill and legs much duller too.

▼ **Females** (middle) are nearly identical to the male, although they lack the red bill knob. **Males** (bottom) have bright red bills, with a knob on the forehead. The plumage is glossier than the females; the green and chestnut deeper toned.

Ruddy Shelduck • *Tadorna ferruginea*

58-70cm, 23-27in

When Occasional spring birds and invaders in late summer and early autumn from near continent. Others in spring **Where** Mainly around coastal marshes and estuaries. Sometimes at inland reservoirs **Confusion species** Egyptian Goose (in flight only) **Call** Nasal honk, also *ang* in flight

An enigmatic bird. No one is really sure if we get wild birds or not, but these Shelduck-sized birds are rather cute!

▲ In flight, shows a startling black and white wing panel, with the black, dark, bottle-green and rufous primaries and trailing edge of the wing. The pale eye patch surround is still seen easily in flight.

◀ A **drake** shows a black neck collar. The upperparts are rich- apricot, with dark wingtips and tail.

Mandarin Duck • *Aix galericulata*

41-49cm, 16-19in

When Throughout the year **Where** Secluded ponds and rivers, mainly in southern England **Confusion species** None **Call** Distinctive whistle

Shy, secretive birds, native to eastern Asia, but have established them-selves as a feral breeding species after introduction from wildfowl collections during the last century.

▲ In flight, **females** (left) appear greyish, with white underparts and white spectacles. **Males** (right) are dark except for white head stripe and orange on cheeks and 'sails'.

◀ **Females** have greyish heads, startling white spectacles. Upperparts dark, with creamy, spotted flanks and chests.

▶ **Males**-WOW! Striking features include a long white eyebrow, orange 'back-combed' face, plum chest, golden flanks and incredible orange 'sails' on the back. The bill is pinkish with a whitish tip.

Eurasian Wigeon • *Anas penelope* 42-50cm, 17-19in

When Arrives from late summer onwards. Leaves in March-April **Where** Coastal marshes, grazing pasture, also inland lakes and reservoirs. Some summer **Confusion species** None **Call** Soft whistled *weee-ooo.*

▶ In flight, **males** (right) show bold-white wing panel. **Females** (left) have a greyish patch on the upperwing, and a rich-buff wash on the flanks. Both share grey underwings.

Medium-sized, plump ducks, with a round head, short neck, shortish-blue bill and pointed tail.

▼ **Females** variable, but have a greyer-looking head than the male. Upperparts duller and forewing greyish. Flanks are generally rich-brown.

▼ **Eclipse male** similar to female, but retains a russet head, grey on the mantle. The white forewing enables you to sex a male, whatever the time of year.

▲ **Males** have russet heads with a yellow central blaze. Upperparts are soft-grey, with darker primaries. Breast is flushed-pink, and the flanks are grey.

Gadwall • *Anas strepera*

46-56cm, 18-22in

When Throughout the year. Numbers increase in late summer to early autumn **Where** Inland waters, but have become increasingly regular on coastal marshes **Confusion species** Mallard (summer only) **Call** Females quack, while males croak a low-pitched *arrgk*

Similar in size to Mallard, but slimmer with narrower wings and body. Have established themselves after introduction in the early 1900s.

◀ **Males** (left) look grey with an obvious white speculum.

▶ **Females** (right) are whiter underneath than Mallard, and the white speculum can be seen from below.

▶ **Females** look less messy than a female Mallard, the bill shows a broad orange edge, with a dark central ridge.Tail tends to be darker than Mallard.

◀ **Males** have a greyish-brown head contrasting with fine, darker-grey vermiculations on the chest (looking like chain-mail). Upperparts are greyish, with brown overlapping scapulars. The white speculum is obvious. Bill is blackish, and the legs, like the female, are orange-yellow.

Common Teal • *Anas crecca*

34-38cm, 13.5-15in

When Throughout the year. Autumn arrivals from August onwards **Where** Coastal lagoons, grazing marshes, reservoirs, gravel pits **Confusion species** Garganey (summer only) **Call** Males have a whistled tree/. Females have a muted *quack*

Small, nervous ducks, which are easily disturbed, taking off vertically from the water. Teals have a delightful display: several males surround a female, throwing their heads back and forth to impress her.

▶ The plum head of the **male** (left) will be easily seen in flight, along with grey-brown wings. **Female** (right) looks grey-brown all over, with the green speculum visible on the wing.

▶ **Females** are mainly grey-brown above, with a white belly. Bill is dark, with variable amounts of orange at the base.

◀ **Males** have a mainly plum-coloured head, with broad-green sides, bordered by cream. Spotted breast is washed yellow, with grey flanks and upperparts. Note the bold, white horizontal line along the middle of the body.

Mallard • *Anas platyrhynchos*

50-60cm, 19.5-23.5in

When Throughout the year **Where** Lakes, ponds, marshes **Confusion species** Gadwall (summer only) **Call** Females have the *quack, quack* call, males give a low nasal whistle

A hefty, large-headed and long-billed dabbling duck, the Mallard is often prone to interbreed with farmyard ducks producing a myriad of pecu- liar-looking offspring.

◀ In flight, **males** (left) show a greyish upperwing, except for the purple speculum. From above, a **female** (right) will look brown and black except for the dark speculum.

▼ **Females** are non-descript birds with brownish upper- and underparts. Note the generally variegated brown and black pattern. Bill is dark brown with orangey edges.

▲ **Males** are unmistakable, with a bottle-green head separated from the rusty-brown breast by a distinctive white neck ring.The tail boasts a couple of curled black feathers, making them look almost ornate.

Pintail • *Anas acuta*

51-62cm, 20-24in

When Mainly from August to March **Where** Coastal marshes, estuaries **Confusion species** None **Call** Rarely heard, a Teal-like *krreew*

An elegant medium-sized duck. Smallish head, slender neck, long, narrow wings and tapered rear end.Breeds in small numbers only.

▼ **Females** look almost demure. Slender appearance, with slim-looking dark slate-blue bill.

▲ In flight, **males** (right) have brown heads with a long, narrow pin-tail. Upperwing is uniform-grey. **Females** (left) have plain upperwings, and a hint of a tapered rear end.

◀ **Males** have chocolate-brown head with white breast and grey upperparts. Long scapulars and tertials cloak the wing. Underparts are grey, with yellow and black towards the rear.

Garganey • *Anas querquedula*

37–41 cm, 14.5-16in

When Arrives from late March onwards, leaves by October **Where** Secluded pools, ditches, often southern and eastern counties **Confusion species** Common Teal **Call** Males have a rattling, frog-like *prrrrrreerup*

A small duck, but larger and bulkier than Teal. Can be hard to separate in early autumn.

▼ **Females** have two dark horizontal 'bars' on the face, lack Teal's green speculum and have a darker tail. Longer, dark bill. Eclipse males and juveniles look similar to females.

▲ In flight, both **male** (left) and **female** (right) have powder-blue to grey forewings and distinctive head patterns.

◀ **Males** have a dark crown with broad white crescents. Face is deep brown, almost maroon-toned. Flanks vermiculated grey and white, rear and breast are spotted brown. Wings show lanceolate grey and black tertials, brown mantle and blackish primaries.

Shoveler • *Anas clypeata*

44-52cm, 17.5-20in

When Year round. More often in autumn and winter **Where** Found on inland and coastal pools or shallow lakes **Confusion species** Shelduck (at distance) **Call** Wooden, rapping *took-took, took-took.*

A chunky, medium-sized duck with a fairly short neck and an amazing- looking bill.

▲ In flight, broad-winged and top-heavy due to the bill. Both sexes have blue or greyish forewings.

▼ **Female's** head pattern similar to female Garganey, but huge bill distinctive. The upper- and underparts are neatly scalloped dark brown.

▶ **Eclipse male** (seen in mid- to late summer) resembles female, except for darker head and rufous-toned flanks.

◀ **Males** in breeding plumage are unmistakable. Note the green head and chestnut flanks. Bill is all black. Be sure to look at the head-bobbing display - it's a must!

Red-crested Pochard • *Netta rufina*

53-57cm, 21in

When Mainly autumn and winter. Feral populations resident. Common escapee **Where** Lakes, ornamental ponds, reservoirs and coastal marshes, mainly southern and eastern Britain **Confusion species** Female Ruddy Duck, Smew, Common Scoter **Call** Mainly silent.

Rather large, heavy-looking birds, with rounded heads and longish bills.

▶ In flight, note the strikingly contrasting upper- and underwing pattern. Both sexes show broad white flashes across the upperwing (males show a little more black on the forewing) and almost entirely white underwings.

▼ **Females** (left) have brownish heads with obvious pale faces. Upperparts are pale brown with buff flanks. Bill is dark grey, often with a pink tip.

◀ **Males** (right) have rich orange-red head, contrasting with brown upperparts and black breast. Flanks are off-white. Coral-red bill is very striking.

Pochard • *Aythya ferina*

42-49cm, 16.5-19in

When Throughout the year, more in winter **Where** Breeds in reedy ditches, marshes and lakes. Large numbers inland during winter **Confusion species** Tufted Duck (females only), Red-crested Pochard **Call** Male's call is a nasal *oooochaa*. Females have a loud *bree-arr*, often heard in flight.

▶ In flight, keep fairly close to water, almost skimming across it. **Males'** (left) red head and greyish upper wings obvious; **females** (right) show a greyish wing panel.

▶ **Female's** face shows pale cream patches and a pale 'spectacle' effect around the eyes. Dark grey bill with a black tip.

Medium-sized ducks, with a sloping forehead, long neck and slightly convex bill. Around 100 pairs breed here every year.

◀ **Males** show a rich, rust-red head, with black breast, white flanks and greyish upperparts. Rear end is black. Black bill shows a grey sub-terminal band.

Ring-necked Duck • *Aythyo collaris*

37-46cm, 14.5-18in

When Mainly autumn and winter, but can be all year **Where** Freshwater ponds, lakes and reservoirs across the country. Mainly south-west England and Ireland **Confusion species** Tufted Duck, Pochard **Call** Vagrants are mainly silent

◀ **Male** similar to Tufted Duck but has different head shape and lacks tuft. Flanks are silvery- grey with a neat white 'spur. The bill shows two white bands, a narrow one at the base and a broader one behind the black tip. Remainder is dark grey-blue.

Rather small, short-bodied birds, with a steep forehead and peaked crown. Known to return to same wintering sites, although some may be escapees from collections.

▶ **Female** is pale brown. Distinct spectacled look and darker, orange eyes. Flank pattern mirrors male, but is fawn-brown with a narrower white 'spur', the bill shows one, broad, white band.

▲ Both sexes resemble **Tufted Duck** (top), but when seen well, you should have little trouble separating them. Note the tail, more pronounced than Tufted Duck.

Ferruginous Duck • *Aythya nycora*

38-42 cm, 15in

When Mainly a winter visitor, others in summer and autumn. Escapees quite common **Where** Sheltered rivers, as well as pools, lagoons and reservoirs **Confusion species** Tufted Duck and *Aythya* hybrids **Call** Female in spring a noisy err, *err*; err, male a sharp *chuk*.

A shy, retiring diving duck, with a short body, and long neck and bill.

◀ In flight, both sexes show a broad white wing flash on the upperwing, and very pale under- wings. Also note the white belly on a flying Ferruginous Duck.

▶ **Females** (top) are browner and duller versions of the richly-coloured male, lacking the deep mahogany tones. Also has dark eyes with brown iris, unlike the white-eyed male.

▼ **Males** (bottom) are deep mahogany-brown on the head and underparts with darker upperparts. The rear end is white, sharply demarcated from the brown flanks. Bill is greyish with pale just behind the dark tip. Note the white eye.

Tufted Duck • *Aythya fuligula*

40-47cm, 16— 18.5in

When Throughout the year **Where** Reedy ditches, freshwater marshes, park lakes, gravel pits and reservoirs **Confusion species** Ring-necked Duck, Greater Scaup, Pochard **Call** Rolling growl - *kkrrrr-kkrrrr-kkrrrr.*

▶ In flight, **males** (right) appear almost black, **females** (left) look brown, but note the broad white wing bar. Flies very quickly, with rapid, rushing wingbeats.

Small diving ducks, with a large head, narrow-looking neck and relatively short body. May form large flocks in winter.

▼ **Females** (top) have a small ragged tuft on crown. Head and breast are dark brown, with a variable white patch at the base of the bill (sometimes prominent, but never like Scaup). Upperparts are uniform brown, with paler flanks.The bill is pale blue, with a dark tip (more obvious than a Greater Scaup).

▼ **Males** (bottom) have dark purple heads (looking green in some lights), with a long crest. Upperparts similar in colour to head. White flanks. Brighter blue bill than female, black tip the same.

Greater Scaup • *Aythya marila*

42-51cm, 20in

When Mainly in late autumn and winter **Where** Offshore and coastal estuaries in northern Britain and Ireland. Also inland in southern England **Confusion species** Tufted Duck **Call** Males are usually silent. Display call similar to Tufted Duck, but lower pitched. Female mirrors the 'growl' of Tufted Duck, but again deeper in tone

◀ **Male** in flight, the larger size of Greater Scaup should be apparent. Both sexes have a broader white wing bar than Tufted Duck.

◀ **Female** in flight superficially resembles Tufted Duck (especially the female), Greater Scaup are bulkier birds, with a large rounded head, bigger bodies and larger

▶ **Males** (front) have a rounded green-coloured head, lacking any hint of a tuft. The head contrasts with the pale back (silvery with fine black vermiculations), white flanks and dark chest. The wings and rear end are black. The bill is a slightly brighter blue than that of the female.

▶ **Females** (back) show a clear white base to the bill and a pale patch on the ear coverts. The

---

Goldeneye • *Bucephala clangula*

40-48cm, I8in

When Mainly in autumn and winter, a few in summer **Where** Breeds around lochs in Scottish Highlands. Elsewhere on pools, lakes, reservoirs **Confusion species** None **Call** Displaying males have a *beeach* noise followed by a Garganey-esque rattle.

Shy, medium-sized diving duck with distinctive head shape and plumage. Also less prone to flock.

◀ In flight, **female** (left) shows limited amount of white on the speculum; **male** (right) shows a lot of white on the upperwing. Legs are pinkish.

▶ **Females'** (back) brown head and piercing yellow eyes are obvious. Triangular bill is blackish with a (variable) yellow tip.

◀ **Males** (front) have a dark green head, with small white patch around lores. Mantle is black and the black scapulars hang over white flanks. Rear end is black in stark contrast with rest of underparts. Bill is wholly black.

Common Eider • *Somateria mollissima* 60–70cm, 28in

When Year round, mainly in winter **Where** Around all coasts. Breeds in northern Britain and Ireland **Confusion species** None **Call** Male Common Eiders have a fabulous, gentle *ooo-ooo-ooo*

▶ In flight, both **male** (left) and **female** (right) share the body bulk, broad wings and triangular-looking head. Eider flocks tend to look rather spread out and straggling. Note how quickly they go by, even in rough weather.

Large, hefty-looking ducks, with a stocky neck, large head and wedge- shaped bill. They favour rocky coastlines, but can also be seen in deeper water off sandier coasts.

▶ **Young males** are often seen offshore in the summer months, well to the south of the breeding range. They show variable plumage, but have a grey head and back, blackish flanks and white chest. The triangular head shape is obvious - due to a steep forehead and longish dull green bill.

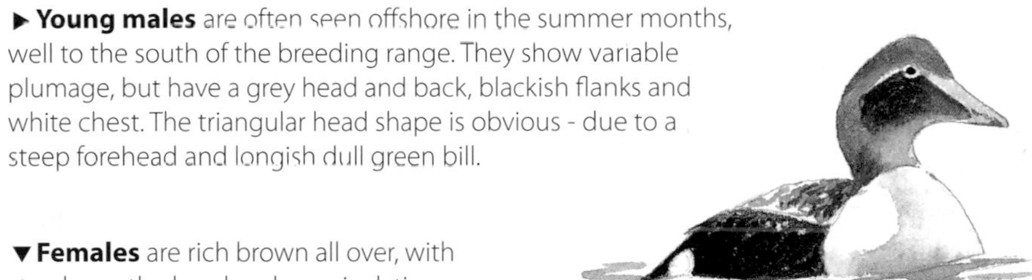

▼ **Females** are rich brown all over, with streaks on the head and vermiculations on the wings and body. The face looks plain. The bill is greyish.

▼ **Males** have a neat black cap, lime green patches on the nape and a pink flush on the breast.

Long-tailed Duck • *Clangula hyernalis* 37-60cm, 23in

When Mainly winter, but some in spring and autumn **Where** Coastal bird around Scotland and Ireland, also England. Rare inland **Confusion species** None **Call** Rarely heard, an Eider-like *00-000*

Small, compact duck with a variety of guises. Have rounded heads, stubby bills and narrow, pointed wings.

◀ In flight, both sexes have white underparts, except for brown breast band. Upperwings grey-brown. Male's tail obvious.

▲ **Breeding males,** black heads with white eye patch. Upperparts blackish, with ginger fringes. Underparts white.

◀ **Non breeding males** (back) have white heads with greyish eye patch and dark cheek spot. A broad brown breast band extends onto mantle, white upperparts. Rest of wing and elongated tail feathers are blackish.

◀ **Females'** (front) head has brown crown and cheek patch. Breast is mottled brown, flanks white.

Common Scoter • *Melanitta nigra* 44-54cm, 21in

When Throughout the year **Where** Breeds on lochs in Scotland and Ireland. Mainly offshore around British coasts. Rare inland **Confusion species** Velvet and Surf Scoter **Call** Male has frequently-repeated, soft *pjeeuw*, in display or after dark. Female has throaty, rattling *grrrro*

A medium-sized sea duck. Often seen in spring on northwards migration, males often return south a couple of months later.

▲ In flight, Scoters are tightly bunched, even in big flocks. Males black, except for pale primaries. Brown and grey heads of females obvious.

◀ **Females** (top) show off-white to grey- brown face and brown crown and nape. Upper- and underparts dark brown. Bill blackish.

◀ **Males** (bottom) black all over. The bill is entirely black, except for a yellow centre. The amount of yellow varies from male to male. Base of bill shows a swollen black knob.

Surf Scoter • *Melanitta perspicillata*

45-56cm, 22in

When Mainly seen in winter, recorded in all seasons **Where** Rare Nearctic vagrant. Mostly offshore in north of Scotland and west coast of Ireland. Recorded in coastal southern England. Even inland records **Confusion species** Common and Velvet Scoter **Call** Silent

▼ **Males** jet-black all over except for two white patches on head and neck. Swollen, tri-coloured bill. Young males are duller, with a grey-white patch on the nape only.

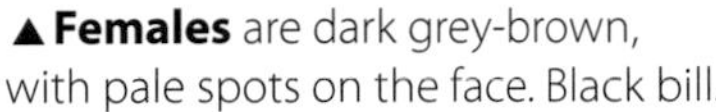

▲ **Females** are dark grey-brown, with pale spots on the face. Black bill.

A North American sea duck seen every year in Britain. Heavier than Common, but slightly smaller than Velvet.

Velvet Scoter • *Melanitta fusca*

51-58cm, 22in

When Mainly in autumn and winter. Some in spring **Where** Entirely coastal around much of the country **Confusion species** Common and Surf Scoter **Call** Silent

▶ In flight, both sexes look dark, both show the characteristic bold white secondaries, visible at some distance.

Clearly larger and bulkier than Common Scoters, with longer bodies, thicker necks and heavy-looking bill.

▶ **Females** (back) dark sooty-brown all over, except for distinctive pale patches on head and lores. White secondaries just visible on birds on sea. Wedge-like bill is greyish.

◀ **Males** (front) are jet-black all over except for a white nick just under the eye and the white secondaries. Bill is mainly yellow-orange with a black centre. Eye is white, both sexes have red feet.

Red-breasted Merganser • *Mergus serrator*

52-58cm, 23in

When All year, particularly in autumn and winter **Where** Breeds on rocky coasts of Scotland and Ireland. Coasts and estuaries in winter **Confusion species** Goosander **Call** Mainly silent

A sawbill, slimmer and smaller-headed than Goosander, with distinctive plumage too.

▲ In flight, brown breast band of a **male** is obvious; the white on the upperwing has more black on it.

▼ **Females** (back) are browner, with more white on upperwing than female Goosander. Female has a thin white loral line and short, untidy-looking crest on the rear crown. Upperparts and flanks are ashy-grey. Red bill with a dark culmen.

▶ **Males** have a green head, and a punk-like crest on the rear crown. The streaked brown chest, stands out against the black and white upperparts and grey flanks.

Goosander • *Mergus merganser*

58—68cm, 23—26.5in

When Mainly in winter, but some in summer **Where** In winter on rivers, estuaries and inland reservoirs in southern Britain. Breeds near water in crevices, mainly in Scotland **Confusion species** Red-breasted Merganser **Call** Males Crane-like echoing call and soft *kuorr*, females a loud *skrrak*.

Large, long-bodied saw- bills, most commonly seen at large winter roosts on big inland reservoirs in England.

◀ **Males** lack brown chest and crested look of female Merganser, more white on the upperwing. Females have grey backs.

▼ **Females** and **juveniles** have neat, deep-brown head, a fuller crest than Red-breasted Merganser and a sharp demarcation between the head and white chest. Also have a whiter throat.

▶ **Males** (bottom) lack the 'punk' look of male Mergansers. Black back, white underparts. Breast often washed pink, flanks can appear cream. Grey tail. Eyes deeper brown than Merganser's.

Smew • *Mergellus albellus*

38–44cm, 15-17in

When Some on passage in autumn, but mainly winter **Where** Inland lakes, reservoirs and gravel pits, mainly southern Britain. Occasionally on coasts **Confusion species** Ruddy Duck, Common Scoter (females only) **Call** Mainly silent

In flight, **males** (right) appear pied, while the greyer **female** (left) will show a contrast between the grey outer wing and white and black inner wing.They are fast fliers and excellent divers.

▼Small, shy 'sawbills' (they have serrated, saw-like edges to the bill and a hooked tip for gripping fish).

▶ **Females** (top) and immatures known as 'redheads'. Head is indeed reddish, but pretty dark, especially around the eye. White face patch and greyish breast and flanks.'Redheads' normally outnumber the males.

▶ **Males** (bottom) look whiter on the water than in flight. These handsome birds show a black loral patch and line on rear of the crown, as well as thin black lines on the breast and flanks. Black mantle, while the flanks are greyish and the tail dark.

Ruddy Duck • *Oxyura jamaicensis*

35-43cm, 14-17in

When Throughout the year **Where** Almost extinct post-eradication. Formerly on inland reservoirs mainly in southern Britain, also coastal marshes and lakes **Confusion species** Common Scoter, Smew (females only) **Call** Displaying males tap their bills against their chest (known as 'bubbling'), causing a low drumming noise

Established in Britain after a few birds escaped from wildfowl collections in the l950s.The population has increased dramatically in recent years.

▶ In flight, **males** (left) are very obvious - white face with russet chest and flanks. **Females** (right) can be told by their large head, face pattern, grey-brown upperparts and white belly.

◀ **Females** (top) show a dark crown, with a pale face and diffuse horizontal stripe under the eye. Broad, slightly convex bill is dark grey with a darker tip.

◀ **Males** have a bold white face patch contrasting strongly with the black head. Upperparts and flanks are reddish. Dark stiff-looking tail. Sky-blue bill with a dark tip.

Red Grouse • *Lagopus lagopus*

33-38cm, 15in

When Throughout the year **Where** Open moorland, only in western and northern Britain, south of Ireland **Confusion species** Black Grouse (female) **Call** In flight, fly off uttering a loud, harsh *krok, krok, krok. The* mating call is *go back, go back, back, back*

Medium-sized, plump gamebird, localised and sedentary. Once Britain's only endemic species, now demoted to a form of Continental Willow Grouse.

◀ In flight, rounded body, small head, broad wings and shortish tail. Wingtips and tail are dark.

◀ **Males** (left) appear dark reddish-brown, with fine black and white vermiculations on the upper- and underparts. Red eyebrows obvious, with white feathered legs and feet. **Females** (right) appear paler and more orange-toned than males. Lack red eyebrows and orbital ring.

Ptarmigan • *Lagopus mutus*

31-35cm, 14in

When Year round **Where** Barren terrain on mountains of northern Scotland **Confusion species** None **Call** A snorting *err-orr kakk-orr*

◀ Similar in size and shape to Red Grouse but slightly smaller and less rotund. **Winter males** almost entirely white. Only markings are black on lores and dark outer tail feather tips. Red eyebrow. Legs have white feathering - like Red Grouse. In summer, males have mottled-grey head, breast and upperparts.

◀ **Females** are intricately marked, a mix of browns, black and white, perfectly camouflaged in mountain heather. Shares the small black bill and black eye of the male, with less obvious red eyebrows. Shows more white in winter, especially on the rump and wings.

Black Grouse • *Tetrao tetrix*

49-58cm, 21 in

When Throughout the year, early spring is best **Where** Open moorland, close to woods/plantations in north Wales, northern England and Scotland **Confusion species** Red Grouse (female) **Call** Greyhens have a cackling *kakakakaka-eh*, males a bubbly *rroo-rrooo-rrooo-per-ooo*

◀ **Females** (Greyhens) similar to female Red Grouse. Less rufous, with hint of a wingbar on upperwing, grey- brown, barred tail, unlike Red Grouse.

▼ **Males** (Blackcocks) stocky in flight. Note white on wings and undertail. Red eyebrows and lyre-shaped tail.

▶ **Males** (middle) display in post-dawn winter and early spring.This is a 'lek', the intention is to pair with a **Greyhen** (right). Several males vie for her attention.

Capercaillie • *Tetrao urogallus*

74-90cm, 29–35in

When Throughout the year, early spring best **Where** Caledonian pine forest in Scottish Highlands **Confusion species** Black Grouse (female only) **Call** Males make a noise likened to 'glugging' from a bottle, followed by a cork popping. Females have a coarse *grack*, often given when perched in trees

A very large game bird, but, despite their size, can be hard to see, often roosting high up in pines.

▶ **Males** are massive (turkey-sized). Head and shaggy throat look dark blackish-blue, with a greener hue to underparts. Huge fanned tail is black, with white flecking. Note large white bill. Can be aggressive, known to attack humans, so be wary of them if you encounter one.

▶ **Females** smaller, with more subdued plumage. Crown and nape are beautifully barred. Face is a plain tawny-brown. The rich ochre breast is unbarred contrasting with the paler barred underparts.

Quail • *Coturnix coturnix*

16-18cm, 7in

When Arrives from early May, calls into August **Where** Open farmland crop fields. Mainly southern and eastern England **Confusion species** Young partridges and Pheasant **Call** A rapid *whip-whi-whip* (sounding like 'wet my lips'

◀ A small, migrant gamebird, numbers vary from year to year. Very hard to see, often hidden in cornfields. May make a brief low, very quick, flight across a cornfield. Note the head pattern in flight.

◀ **Females** (back) similar to males, but far less pronounced head pattern, and no black on throat. Breast is often more flecked and spotted than male.

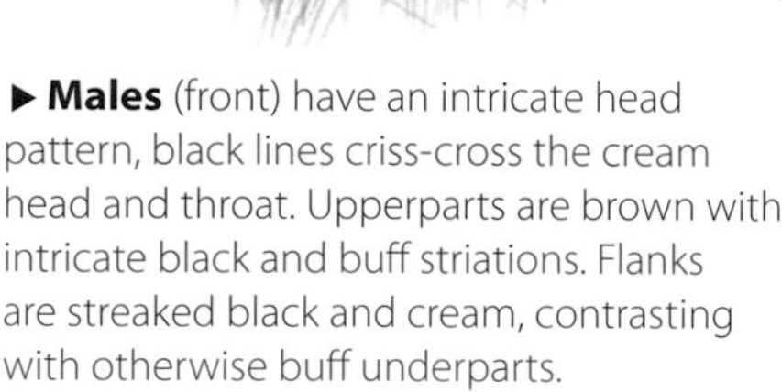

▶ **Males** (front) have an intricate head pattern, black lines criss-cross the cream head and throat. Upperparts are brown with intricate black and buff striations. Flanks are streaked black and cream, contrasting with otherwise buff underparts.

Grey Partridge • *Perdix perdix*

28-32cm, 12in

When Throughout the year **Where** Open farmland with hedgerows across much of the country **Confusion species** Red-legged Partridge **Call** A rasping *kerri-ick,* most often heard at dusk.

▼ **Juveniles** (back) have brown heads (darker on the crown and eye-stripe), buff breast, upperparts. Flanks streaked with fine white and black lines.

A stocky, plump medium-sized game bird, often in groups.The species has suffered a dramatic decline in the past two decades.

◀ **Females** have a much reduced belly patch, and look a little duller than males.

◀ **Males** (far left) have neat brick-red face, with a brown crown, grey throat and breast. Large brown belly patch and rusty flank stripes.

Red-legged Partridge • *Alectoris rufa*

32–36cm, 14in

When Throughout the year **Where** Mainly farmland, also heaths, dunes in England **Confusion species** Grey Partridge **Call** Loud, rasping *chuck, chuck, chuckak*

A rounder-looking bird than the Grey Partridge, often appears more upright than Grey.They also show a more striking head pattern, plainer back and more complex underpart markings than the scarcer Grey.

▶ Fly quickly and low on bowed-looking wings. Note the two-tone wings and orange tail sides. 'Red-legs' habitually run more than they fly (certainly less inclined to fly than Greys).

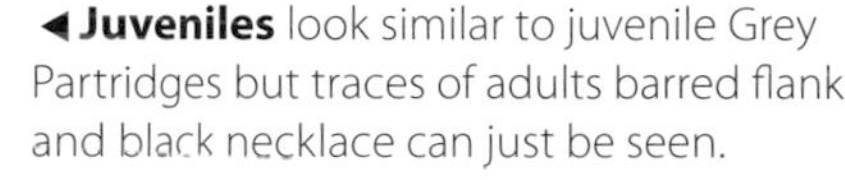

◀ **Juveniles** look similar to juvenile Grey Partridges but traces of adults barred flanks and black necklace can just be seen.

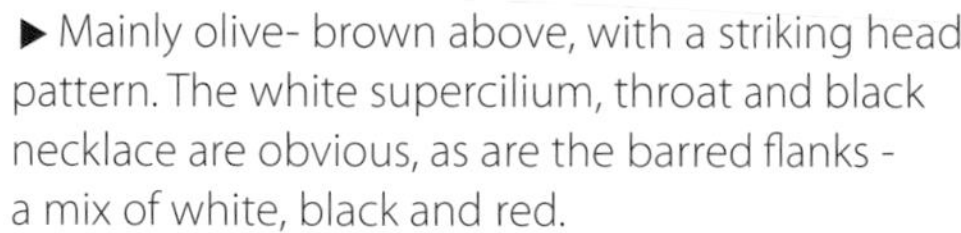

▶ Mainly olive- brown above, with a striking head pattern. The white supercilium, throat and black necklace are obvious, as are the barred flanks - a mix of white, black and red.

Pheasant • *Phasianus colchicus*

70-90cm, 27-35in

When Throughout the year **Where** Woodland, farmland, marshes and even in reedbeds across the country **Confusion species** Golden and Lady Amherst's Pheasant **Call** Distinctive, rapid fire *kutuk, kutuk, kutuk*

▶ Characteristic flight. Fast, whirring wingbeats interrupted by a glide. Cannot sustain flight for long.

An unmistakable, long-tailed gamebird, introduced into some areas of Europe, from Asia, as many as 2000 years ago. They have been present in northern Europe for over 200 years.

▼ **Males** also variable. The deep bottle-green head and 'ear tufts' contrast with the obvious patch red facial skin. Mantle is a rich orange-red colour, variably blotched and spotted with cream, black and white. The long, spiky tail is warm-brown, with copper-toned outer feathers. Central feathers show thin, broadly spaced bars to the tip.

▲ ◀ **Females** are highly variable birds. Generally buff-grey-brown all over with barring on the head, upper- and underparts, they are always smaller, slighter and shorter tailed than males.

Golden Pheasant • *Chrysolophus pictus*

90-105cm, 35-41 in

When Throughout the year **Where** Mixed and conifer woodland. Colonies in south-west Scotland, southern and eastern England **Confusion species** Lady Amherst's and Common Pheasant (females only) **Call** Male has a harsh, piercing *ehk* or *ehk-aik*.

An introduced, exotic species, native to central China. Introduced in the late 1800s, a few colonies still exist.

▶ **Females are** barred all over, and tend to be a rich / ginger-brown tone.

▶ **Males,** a rather gaudy affair and unmistakable. Curiously, despite its multi-coloured look, they can be very hard to see, often best looked for in the early morning.

Lady Amherst's Pheasant • *C. amherstiae*

112cm, 44in

When Throughout the year **Where** Confined to just a single location in Bedfordshire. Woodland with dense undergrowth **Confusion species** Golden and Common Pheasant (females only) **Call** Heard towards dusk *aaak, aek-aek*

Originates from montane areas of China. Like Golden Pheasant, it was introduced to Britain in the early 1900s.

▶ **Males** are spectacular creatures and unmistakable, with a multi-coloured body and an incredibly long tail, which is delicately marked black and white. They are secretive birds and hard to see.

Head and upper body are black and scalloped white, with stark white belly and flanks. Upperparts are a dazzling rainbow of colours, deep green mantle, cerulean blue wings, with yellow and red on back and rump. Females resemble Golden Pheasant, but are larger and darker with a barred (rather than plain) rump. The tail is longer with bolder bars.

Red-throated Diver • *Gavia stellata*

55-67cm, 23in

When Throughout the year **Where** Breeds on Scottish lochs. Others offshore, around all coasts. Rare inland **Confusion species** Black-throated and Great Northern Diver **Call** In flight, a goose-like *cah-cah-cah.* Breeding males' song is an eerie *oo-rrrooo-oh, oo-rrrooo-oh* while the females' is a high-pitched *arroo-arroo-arroo*

◀ **Breeding** birds (left) show a dove-grey head, contrasting with the red throat. Fine black and white streaks extend from the top of the head onto the sides of the breast and flanks.

▼ **Juveniles** are grey-brown around the head and throat, with scaly-looking back and wings.

▲ **Non breeding** birds (above) show dark top of head and neck contrasting with white face and throat. Back and wings more speckled, with darker flecks on flanks.

Black-throated Diver • *Gavia arctica*

63-75cm, 23in

When Year round **Where** Breeds on freshwater lakes, sea lochs in Scotland. Otherwise offshore. Rare inland **Confusion species** Red-throated Diver **Call** A harsh *knar-knar.* Song is a loud, solitary noise - a rising, whistled *kloee-ko-kloee-ko-kloee*

▼ **Non breeding** birds (below) black and white (beware - Red-throated can look very black and white!). Obvious white flank patch towards the birds' rear end.

◀ **Breeding** birds' (left) head and nape are grey, contrasting with 'pinstripes' on the side of neck and a jet black throat. The upperparts are black with bold white chequers. The white flank patch is still obvious.

◀ **Juveniles** resemble adult winters but greyer overall, with distinctive scaling on the upperparts. When relaxed' and sitting high in the water, white flank patch is seen easily.

Great Northern Diver • *Gavia immer*

73-88cm, 32in

When Mainly in winter, a few seen in spring and autumn **Where** Generally offshore on western coasts. Scarcer on east coast. Rare inland **Confusion species** Black-throated and Red-throated Diver **Call** Atmospheric, eerie almost laughing *ho-yeyeyeyeyeyaaa.* Song is similar to Black-throated Diver - a wailing *aaaoh-we-we-a-we-we-a*

▶ **Non breeding** birds show a large, hefty, silvery bill (obviously larger than the other two divers) and distinctive double peak to the head. Head and upperparts are blackish. Face is white, as are the remainder of the underparts.

▼ **Juveniles** are grey-brown, with lightly-scaled upperparts. Bill shows a dark culmen and tip.

▲ **Breeding** birds (front) have a black head, with a slash of black and white barring on the throat, barred upper flanks. The upperparts are boldly chequered white on black, while the flanks and rear end are black, with white flecking. The thick, heavy bill is black.

Little Grebe • *Tachybaptus ruficollis*

23-29cm, 10in

When Throughout the year **Where** Vegetated waterways, from inland reservoirs to coastal marshes **Confusion species** Black-necked and Slavonian Grebe **Call** High-pitched call (sounding like a cartoon *tee-hee-hee)* is a repeated *bi-bi-bi-bi-bi-bi-bi.*

◀ **Juveniles** have broad brown to black stripes on the side of the neck. Upperparts are brownish, with buff flanks and a fluffy, white rear.

Shy birds. The smallest of the British grebes with short, straight bills, unlike other small grebes.

▶ **Non breeding** birds have a brown crown with a buff face and neck. Upperparts are dark brown, with buff flanks and white rear end. Adult bill is pinkish, with a pale yellow gape spot.

◀ **Breeding** adults have a dark crown with a deep chestnut face and throat. Flanks are dark brown, rear end is white and often puffed up. Bill is small and black, with a bright yellow spot at the base. In flight, Little Grebes show no white on the wing.

Great Crested Grebe • *Podiceps cristatus*

46-51 cm, 19in

When Year round. Migrants in autumn **Where** Breeds on large, open well-vegetated water. Passage birds at sea **Confusion species** Red-necked Grebe, Red-throated Diver **Call** Variety of harsh sounding noises including a far carrying *kraa-ahhar* and *krrow*

Our largest grebe, identified by their longish,thin neck, long slim body and distinctive plumage.

◀ **Juveniles** (rear) retain black neck stripes for some while. Dark crown, extends to dark upperparts. Underparts are dark greyish-brown, with a white rear end. Slim, dagger-like bill is a dull pinkish-brown.

▲ **Non breeding** adults have a dark crown and nape, with plain white face. Upperparts are dark brown, underparts show greyish- brown flanks and white rear end.

▼ **Breeding** adults are unmistakable. Head has dark ear tufts, while the sides of the head are chestnut, merging to blackish side plumes, fanned in courtship. Chicks sit on the female's back. In flight, the fore- and rear- wings are white. Courtship is an elaborate routine of head-to-head shaking and bobbing, climaxing in an amazing dance across the water.

Red-necked Grebe • *Podiceps grisegena*

40–46cm, 16in

When Mainly autumn and winter, scarce in spring **Where** Coastal bays and estuary mouths, mainly east and south coasts. Rare inland **Confusion species** Great Crested Grebe **Call** Mainly silent. In summer, a loud *cherk* is most likely to be heard

Red-necked Grebes are stockier and slightly smaller than Great Crested Grebes, with shorter bills. Chunkier and thicker set than the three smaller grebe species.

▶ **Breeding** birds are very striking. The black cap contrasts with the white face patch and rich red neck. Stout bill is bi-coloured, black towards the tip, yellow at base.

▶ **Juveniles** show black stripes across the white face patch, with a reddish-brown neck.The rest of the plumage is much like an adult winter.

▼ **Non breeding** adults retain a dark cap, but the face is sullied grey. Neck is generally buff- brown.The rest of the under parts and upperparts are as the summer adult.

Slavonian Grebe • *Podiceps auritus* 31-38cm, 12.5in

When Throughout the year **Where** Breeds on small Scottish pools and lakes. Mainly coastal in autumn/winter **Confusion species** Black-necked and Little Grebe **Call** Far carrying *hy-arrr* and, while displaying, a laughing trill

Slightly larger and stockier than the Little Grebe, but always check the bill and head shapes of winter birds.

▲**Juveniles** resemble non breeding adults, but tend to show a mottled dusky cheek bar.

▲**Non breeding** birds have a sloping black forehead and peaked crown, with white face and throat. Flanks are blackish, fading to grey, with a white rear end. Short, brown bill with black tip. Back of head looks white, with a thin, black central stripe.

◀**Breeding** birds have jet-black heads with striking golden fans on the sides. Underparts are dull rusty-red, fading to white on the tail. Upperparts are dark grey. Pale tip on dark bill.

Black-necked Grebe • *Podiceps nigricollis* 31-38cm, 12.5in

When Throughout the year **Where** Breeds in small numbers, on shallow ponds around Britain and Ireland. In winter around coasts and inland waters **Confusion species** Slavonian and Little Grebe **Call** Rarely heard, a short *vit* and a rising *pu-iey*

A scarce, small grebe, with a rounded head and distinctive bill shape. Stockier than Slavonian Grebe.

▼**Juveniles'** head pattern similar to non breeding adults, but show a brown wash to the cheeks and throat. Pale base to bill.

▲**Breeding** bird's whole head and neck is black, with obvious golden ear tufts. Upperparts are blackish, with rusty-red underparts and a pale rear. Less puffed up at rear than either Slavonian or Little Grebe. Small, black bill is distinctly up-turned, unlike Slavonian.

▶**Non breeding** birds easily confused with winter Slavonians. Black cap extends onto white cheeks into a dark smudge below eye. Throat has a greyish wash, fading to the flanks.

Gannet • *Morus bassanus*

85-97cm, 36in

When On breeding grounds by early spring. Passage birds year round, mostly autumn **Where** Colonies off Scottish coasts and northern England. Otherwise at sea. Rare inland **Confusion species** Large shearwaters (autumn only) **Call** A loud grating while breeding; silent at sea

▲ A large seabird, with a strong head, powerful bill, long angled-looking wings and wedge-shaped tail. **Juveniles** (far left) show almost wholly dark grey-brown plumage, with distinctive pale horseshoe rump patch. **Second year** birds (centre left) have white heads and begin to show white on the wings.

▲ **Third year** birds (centre right) have an almost fully-white head, with a yellow wash. Wings and mantle are mixed white on black. Tail remains dark. **Fourth year** birds (far right) have an adult-like wing pattern, except for black flecks across the wing. Tail is almost wholly white.

▼ The flying **adult** (rear) shows black only on the wingtips, unlike the immatures. Flies on quick, shallow beats, with short glides. Resemble giant shearwaters as they career through the waves.

▼ This nesting **adult** shows a yellow wash to the head, contrasting with snow-white body. Wingtips are black. Notice the pale silver dagger of a bill and black eye patch.

Fulmar • *Fulmarus glacialis*

43-52cm, 18.5in

When Throughout the year **Where** Breeds on ledges and cliffs, also buildings. Pelagic for rest of year. Rare inland **Confusion species** Cory's and Great Shearwater **Call** Can be noisy, lots of guttural cackles

◀ In flight, glides along on stiff, straight wings, interspersed with series of shallow, rapid wing beats. Underwing white with thin dark border, more prominent towards the wingtip.

Reminiscent of a small Herring Gull, these are thickset-looking birds. Don't get too close to them though - they have a habit of vomiting foul-smelling oil on you!

▶ **Adults** have rounded head, with large black eyes. Upperparts grey, with darker-looking primaries. Grey rump and tail. Most obvious feature is amazing 'tubenose' - the yellowish, slightly-hooked bill is topped by pale blue tube, used to filter salt from seawater - a feature shared with albatrosses, shearwaters and petrels.

Cory's Shearwater • *Calonectris diomedia*

45-56cm, 22in

When From late July until mid-September. Occasional summer and late autumn records **Where** Entirely coastal, mainly south-west England and Ireland, occasionally east coast **Confusion species** Great Shearwater, Gannet, Fulmar **Call** Silent

◀ From below, notice unmarked white underparts, dark trailing hindwing and wingtips. Head shows distinctive grey shawl effect. A large shearwater with brown and white plumage and distinctly bowed-looking wings. Occasionally seen in very high numbers in late July and early August.

◀ From above, wings appear dark brown, with dark grey uppertail,'saddle' and head. Can show pale horseshoe on the rump, never as pronounced as Great Shearwater. At close range, note the yellowish bill.

◀ Relaxed flight action frequently includes long glides. The distinctive shape is apparent to practised eyes, even at great distance.

Great Shearwater • *Puffinus gravis*

43-51 cm, 20in

When From late July into October. Occasional late autumn records **Where** Entirely coastal, mainly south-west England and Ireland. Very rare on east coast. Breeds in south Atlantic **Confusion species** Cory's Shearwater, Gannet, Fulmar **Call** Silent

Slightly smaller and slimmer-looking than Cory's, with stiffer, more rapid wing beats and darker-looking plumage. Also, occasionally seen in high numbers during late summer.

▶ Upperparts almost entirely dark brown, with delicate, pale fringing. Close up, dark cap and whitish collar can be seen. White horseshoe rump patch and blackish tail obvious. Bill appears thinner and blacker than Cory's Shearwater.

◀ The underside is quite different from Cory's Shearwater. Note dark markings across underwing, darkish belly patch and brownish 'thumbprint' mark on the shoulder. The head looks capped.

Sooty Shearwater • *Puffinus griseus*

40-50cm, 16in

When Mainly autumn, rare at other times of the year **Where** Always seen at sea, mainly on west and east coasts in rough weather **Confusion species** Balearic Shearwater, Arctic Skua, young Gannet **Call** Silent

Medium- to large-sized dark shearwater, clearly bigger than Manx Shearwater. Sooty Shearwaters have narrow-looking, slightly swept-back wings.

▶ Obvious silvery panel on underwings contrasting with sooty-brown belly, more distinct than the similar Balearic Shearwater. Upperside is sooty-brown, or black in bad light.

▶ Note shape of the body and tapering rear end and wedge-shaped tail. 'Sooties' are powerful flyers, rarely struggling, even in very rough weather.

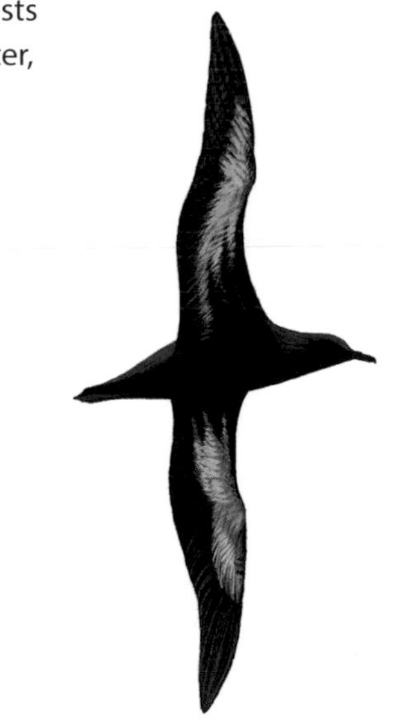

Manx Shearwater • *Puffinus puffinus* 30-35cm, 14in

When At breeding sites from early spring, leaving in early autumn. Passage birds in spring and autumn **Where** Breeds in burrows around west coast of Britain and Ireland. Passage birds around all coasts **Confusion species** Balearic and Sooty Shearwater **Call** At the burrow, a loud *chee-ke ga-ach*, a bit like clearing your throat

◀ Flies with glides and few flaps in rough weather, in calmer conditions they fly low over the water, with shallow beats on stiff wings. Powerful flyers, rarely struggling, even in very rough weather.

◀ Head has dark patch around eye and dark smudge on shoulder. Underside white, except for dark edge to the wing. Upperparts blackish, appearing brown in sunlight. The distinctive head and breast patches can be seen.

They return to their burrows under cover of darkness, negotiating their way by call.

Balearic Shearwater • *Puffinus mauretanicus* 34-39cm, 15in

When Late spring and early summer, through to late autumn **Where** Coastal, mainly off south and south-west coasts of England. Rare elsewhere **Confusion species** Manx and Sooty Shearwater **Call** Silent

◀ Upperside sooty-brown or black in bad light. Note shape of the body and tapering rear end and wedge-shaped tail.

▲ Underside has dark markings on 'armpit', with off- white underwing. Belly appears similar, although this is variable. Lower belly and ventral area always dark. Head is dark, with paler throat.

▲ From above, rather chocolate-brown when compared to Manx Shearwater and a shade lighter than the larger, more angular Sooty Shearwater - only apparent in optimum light, which is seldom seen when seawatching! Some paleness on the upper breast may be seen, while dumpy, short-tailed rear end will be dark.

Storm-petrel • *Hydrobates pelagicus*

15-16cm, 6in

When Returns to breeding sites in early spring. Passage birds mainly late summer to early winter **Where** Breeds in burrows off Scottish and Irish coasts, also far southwest. Otherwise at sea **Confusion species** Leach's Storm-petrel **Call** From inside the burrow, they give a deep purr, coupled with grunts

The smallest member of the family, resembling a fluttery House Martin as they fly through the waves.

◀ Occasionally stops to flutter, before heading off with brief glides and shears into another trough.

◀ Small black head and thin 'tubenose' bill. Mantle and rounded wings also black. Rump is white U-shape, extending onto underside. Tail squared-off, with rounded corners.

▲ Underparts black, except for white rump sides. Most obvious feature is the broad white bar on the underwing.

Leach's Storm-petrel • *Oceanodroma leucorhoa*

18-21cm, 8.5in

When At breeding sites by mid-May. More frequently seen in autumn gales **Where** Breeds on remote islands off Scotland and Northern Isles. Passage birds coastal, mainly north-west England **Confusion species** Storm-petrel **Call** Cooing, with high pitched *wooe-cha*

▶ Angled, pointed wings with distinctive pale grey-brown panel across upperwing. Shape of white on rump appears V-shaped, with a hint of grey through the centre. White rump doesn't wrap around quite like it does on Storm-petrel. Tail shows a notch, or fork.

Larger, longer-winged bird than Storm-petrel, with different plumage and flight action. Fairly powerful glides and shears in gusty weather, often holding position before veering off with powerful beats.

▲ Underparts sooty-black, with a hint of white extending down from rump. Plain underwings.

Great Cormorant • *Phalacrocorax carbo* 77-94cm, 37in

When Year round **Where** Nests around western and northern coasts. Inland in south-east and Midlands **Confusion species** Shag **Call** Noisy at nest sites, a variety of deep, guttural calls

A large bird, with a heavy-looking bill, large, square head and roundish body. Continental birds more like Shags.

Many areas of Britain and Ireland now host the Continental form of Cormorant ***(sinensis).*** These are smaller, more Shag-like birds, which have a slimmer-looking bill, a different pattern of yellow facial skin (showing less than British ***carbo'***s) and appear more Shag-like in flight. Many ***sinensis*** now breed through eastern England and the Midlands. Mixed colonies becoming more frequent.

Juvenile (left) markedly different from the **breeding plumaged adult** (right). The plumage lacks all the green and copper tones - brown upperparts contrast with the very pale off-white underparts.

▲Cormorants in full **breeding** plumage look magnificent! The green sheen of the head and underparts contrasts with the copper-toned wings. Show white flecking on the back of the head. The bill is broad and heavy-looking. Notice the yellow facial skin and lovely, light blue eye colour.

Shag • *Phalacrocorax aristotelis*

68-78cm, 36in

When Throughout the year **Where** Breeds along west coast of Britain and Ireland. Rarer off east coast **Confusion species** Great Cormorant **Call** Grunts and hissing while nesting

Shags are smaller and less bulky than Cormorants, with steep foreheads, small heads and slimmer bills. They often nest on seaweed-strewn crevices and boulders.

▲ In flight, **Cormorants** (left) look large and bulky, with a distinctive neck kink. Wings look broad and the tail relatively short. **Shags** (right) look neat and slim, with narrower wings and longer tail. They also tend to fly lower over water with faster beats and fewer glides.

▼ **Non breeding** birds (left) and **juvenile** Shags (right) show the distinctive head shape and slimmer bill. The yellow patch at the base of the bill is a different shape. Non breeding Shags are dark green, while the juvenile shows more brown on the underparts than a young Cormorant, and the wings look almost barred.

▶ **Adult** Shags are metallic green all over, looking shiny in sunlight. Note the funky-looking teddyboy quiff!

White Stork • *Ciconia ciconia*

95-110cm, 40in

When Genuine wild birds appear between April-June, occasionally in autumn
Where Favours farmland and marshes, mainly southern Britain. Many escapes at large
Confusion species Grey Heron, Common Crane (at distance) **Call** Virtually silent

Look huge in flight and rather graceful on the ground.

▲ In flight, the size of the White Stork is something to behold, looking graceful and elegant as they soar. Note the ultra-distinctive black and white pattern of the upper- and underwing. The neck and legs are held outstretched, unlike Grey or Purple Heron, but just like Common Crane.

▼ Very large with characteristic red legs and bill, along with black and white plumage

▲ On the ground, nothing looks like a White Stork. The pied plumage stands out, as does the bright red of the thick bill and longish legs. Younger birds are duller with less-bright bare parts.

Spoonbill • *Platalea leucorodia*

80-93cm, 31-36in

When Mainly in spring, with some autumn passage. One breeding colony in East Anglia. Some overwinter. **Where** In spring, mainly along east coast, autumn birds in south too. Winters regularly in far south-west **Confusion species** None **Call** Juveniles 'trill' at adults

▲ **Juveniles** have black wing tips and pink-looking bills. A flying Spoonbill holds its head and neck out stretched, with legs trailing behind. Spoonbills are pretty fast flyers, fairly quick, shallow beats sees them cover distance easily.

A tall bird, with a fairly small body. Bred in Britain in 1998 for the first time in over 200 years. Spring flocks are not uncommon.

◀ **Breeding** birds are very handsome.The breast shows a distinctive yellow band across it. Note the crest and, of course, the amazing yellow-tipped bill.

Common Bittern • *Botaurus stellaris*

70-80cm, 29.5in

When Throughout the year **Where** Breeds in large reedbeds, mainly East Anglia, other sites across Britain. Migrants at freshwater pools **Confusion species** Grey and Purple Heron **Call** Once heard, you will never forget the boom of a Common Bittern. Sounds like someone blowing over the top of a bottle

▼A stocky, medium-sized heron, very shy When alarmed, a Common Bittern will stretch its neck up in alarm, and tilt its bill skyward.

▶Smaller and more compact than Grey Heron, flies with quick wing beats with its greenish legs trailing behind. Head shows black cap and moustachial stripe, with white throat and streaked breast sides.

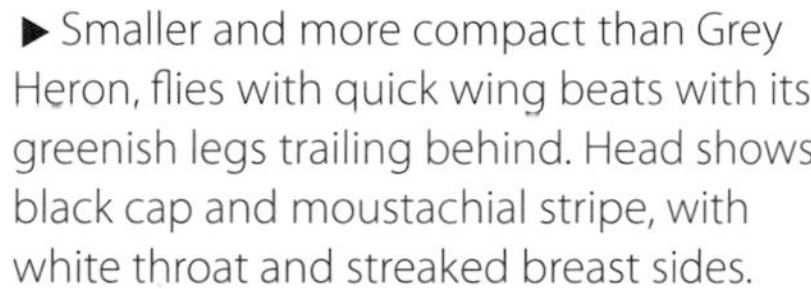

◀Sometimes emerges on the edge of a reedbed to feed. Head pattern and thick, greenish bill are striking. Upperparts are brown, with black vermiculations - dark feather centres with brown fringes and edges.

Little Egret • *Egretta garzetto*

55-65cm, 23-24in

When Throughout the year **Where** Coastal estuaries, marshes, lakes and rivers, increasingly inland. Breeds across southern Britain, also Ireland **Confusion species** Spoonbill, rarer egrets **Call** A nasal *ksheeh* and a soft *raak*

A medium-sized, all-white heron. Formerly a rare spring visitor to Britain, they now breed at several sites and, in summer, roosts of hundreds are not unusual.

▶In flight, Little Egret holds its neck hunched up with its legs trailing like a Grey Heron.They gener-ally fly slowly, with deep beats - but can be pretty quick if spooked.

◀**Breeding** birds have fine aigrettes on the head, breast and back.The straight, dagger-like bill is black, with a yellow base.The legs are black, with yellow feet. **Non breeding** birds lack the plumes and have paler-looking bills. **Juveniles** are similar, but have variable leg and feet colour.

Grey Heron • *Ardea cinerea*

84-102cm, 33-40in

When Year round **Where** Nests in trees, close to water. Lakes, rivers, marshes and estuaries **Confusion species** Purple Heron, Common Bittern **Call** In flight, a loud, hard *frank* or *kkrrank*

Tall, slender, elegant birds with a heavy-looking, dagger like bill, long legs and grey, white and black plumage.

▲ In flight, Grey Herons look big. They fly slowly on bowed wings, with their neck held hunched and their long legs trailing beyond the tail.

▶ Communal nesters, favouring woodland trees as breeding sites, but they will also breed in reedbeds and, occasionally, on cliffs.

◀ **Juveniles** (right) slightly stockier than **adults** (left) and always darker, usually grey, but often mixed with brown. Note the differences in head and bill patterns.

◀ **Adult** shows two broad, black stripes over the back of the crown. In the breeding season, these extend into slim, black head plumes. Upperparts are blue-grey, with a distinctive black shoulder and pale, silvery plumes over the upper part of the closed wing.

Purple Heron • *Ardea purpurea*

70-90cm, 27.5-35in

When Most commonly spring overshoot, but many autumn records **Where** Reedbeds, damp meadows, mainly in southern Britain **Confusion species** Grey Heron **Call** Barked kreck, shorter and less resonant than Grey Heron

Purple Herons are rather lanky- looking birds and, compared to Grey Heron, look darker with a slimmer, longer bill, narrower neck and different flight profile. When seen clearly, plumage is striking and differences are obvious.

▲In flight, will appear rather dark (but beware melanistic Grey Heron), with a more angular look to the snaky neck. The wings can appear a little more angled and the flight almost jerky. The legs and feet are often said to resemble a bundle of sticks, unlike Grey's.

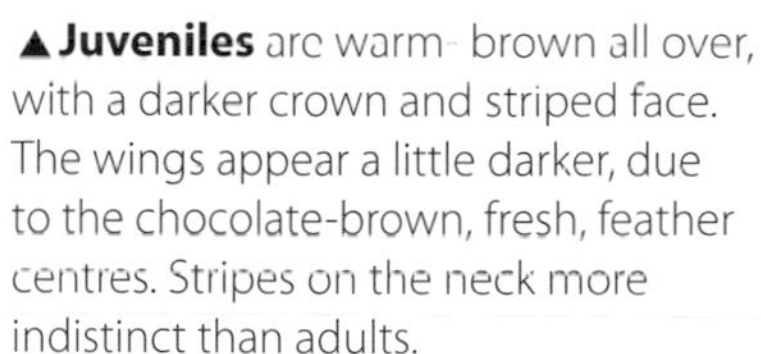

▲**Juveniles** are warm- brown all over, with a darker crown and striped face. The wings appear a little darker, due to the chocolate-brown, fresh, feather centres. Stripes on the neck more indistinct than adults.

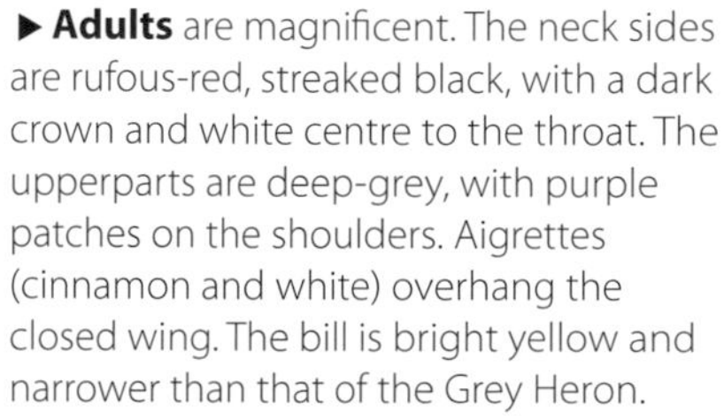

▶ **Adults** are magnificent. The neck sides are rufous-red, streaked black, with a dark crown and white centre to the throat. The upperparts are deep-grey, with purple patches on the shoulders. Aigrettes (cinnamon and white) overhang the closed wing. The bill is bright yellow and narrower than that of the Grey Heron.

Red Kite • *Milvus milvus*

61-72cm, 24-28in

When Present throughout the year **Where** generally found around woodland near open fields, but have expanded to becoming a suburban dweller too. The Welsh countryside is where truly "pure" British stock remains, while reintroduced birds from Scandinavia have established themselves, incredibly successfully, across many parts of England, Scotland and Ireland and are now a couple of "wild" generations into breeding success **Confusion species** Common Buzzard and the rare, vagrant Black Kite **Call** Seldom heard, often mew softly, not unlike a Common Buzzard

◀ From below, note the obvious pale panels on the underwing, which contrast strongly with the black wingtips and carpal patches.The contrast between the forewing and the rear wing is striking too. Tail can sometimes appear to have only a shallow fork, especially when fully fanned, at other times, the deep notch is obvious. From above, the upperwing shows a pale buffy bar across the wing coverts, contrasting with the reddish forewing and blackish hindwing. The rich red tones of the tail (duller on younger birds) are easily seen and good views will show the blackish tail corners and fine white tip.

▶ Seeing a perched Red Kite isn't as tough nowadays as it once was. Note the finely streaked grey head that contrasts with the deep reddish-brown upper- and underparts. The long dark wingtips rest on the longer tail, and note too the strong, yellow legs and feet and also the yellow bill with its black tip.

Honey Buzzard • *Perm's apivorus* 52-59cm, 20.5-23in

When Arrive from May onwards. Passage birds in spring and autumn **Where** Breeds in a tiny number of locations in Britain. Passage birds mainly on east coast **Confusion species** Common Buzzard **Call** Silent, except breeding birds who utter a whistled *pee-u*

A highly-variable species, larger and longer-winged than Common Buzzard, with a small-looking head.

◀ **Males** look greyer above and paler below than **females.** Note here the different underpart markings of these males. Left-hand bird more typical, while the bird on the right shows more dark on the underwing.

▶ In flight long-winged and long-tailed when gliding, and head on look as though they have down-curved wings.

▲ Small head and long tail are distinctive with a good view.

White-tailed Eagle • *Haliaeetus albicilla* 76-92cm, 36in

When Breeding birds all year, vagrant in late autumn/winter **Where** Breeds on Inner Hebrides, also mainland Scotland.Vagrants mainly east coast **Confusion species** Golden Eagle **Call** A continuous *kyick, kyick, kyick*

Huge birds on the ground (like a mini-haystack), they seem vast in flight, with long broad wings, long neck and short tailed. Reintroduced to Inner Hebrides, there is now a thriving (but small) population there, and its range is slowly expanding.

▶ **Immatures** lack the white tail of adult birds, but are no less impressive. They are almost entirely brown above and below, with varying degrees of paleness on the upper- and underwing. Some pale may be seen on the shafts of the tail in some lights. The huge bill is yellow with a large, dark tip.

▲ In good light, the **adult's** underparts appear almost straw-coloured, contrasting with the darker underwing. Wedge-shaped tail is white, sometimes hard to see. Big, heavy yellow bill can often be seen in flight. Watching crows and gulls mob this vast bird is a sight to behold!

Marsh Harrier • *Circus aeruginosas*

43-55cm, 17-21 in

When Throughout the year **Where** Breeds in reedbeds and crop fields in East Anglia. Widespread migrant, winters in east **Confusion species** Common and Honey Buzzard, other harriers (male only) **Call** Females have a thin whistle. Male's display call is a nasal *wav-ee*

A large raptor, bigger than a Buzzard, always appears heavier and broader-winged than Hen and Montagu's Harriers.

▶ **Juveniles** and **females** (left and right) look dark, chocolate-brown all over except for paler-looking underwings and variable amounts of cream markings on the head and forewing.

◀ **Male** (left) in flight, Marsh Harriers often have their wings held in a shallow V-shape, but are also capable of soaring to great heights. Display flight is characterised by plunging and tumbling, often from a great height.

▶ When perched notice the pale head of the **male.** Generally brown upperparts, and grey upperwings and tail.

▶ **Males** from below have a pattern of black, grey and brown, slightly reminiscent of a Red Kite or Montagu's Harrier.

Hen Harrier • *Circus cyaneus*

45-55cm, 21 in

When Mainly in winter, some summer **Where** Increasingly threatened breeding species on northern moors. Winters in open country, moorland and coastal sites **Confusion species** Montagu's Harrier **Call** Rarely heard, females whistle when receiving food and chatter when alarmed. Males *chek* or *chuck*

Slightly smaller than the Marsh Harrier, lighter in build and flight, plumage also markedly different.

▶ **Males** show inky-black wingtips, white underwings, greyish chest and undertail. Ghostly from above, with white rump patch.

▶ **Males** have grey head and upperparts, except for black wings. Grey breast merges into a white belly.

▶ **Females** look brown above and streaked below. Face pattern distinctive. May show a white rump patch and barred tail, hence the term 'ringtail'.

Montagu's Harrier • *Circus pygargus*

39–50cm, 15–19in

When From early May. Breeding birds leave by early September **Where** Breeds (very rare) in open arable land, mainly in eastern Britain. Passage birds anywhere **Confusion species** Hen Harrier, Marsh Harrier (male only) **Call** Rarely heard

Sleek and slender, with long, narrow wings, slim body and a narrow, long tail.

▶ **Females** and **juveniles** look quite similar. Underwing looks barred, browner on the forewing. Belly is streaked and tail barred. Upperside shows mainly brown plumage, except for the pale covert bar, and the slim white rump patch, not as prominent as female/juvenile Hen Harriers.

▶ ▼ **Males** have dark grey wings, with a black band, black wingtips and narrow white rump. From below, the wingtips remain black. Note the thick black bars and finer rufous streaks on underwing.

Sparrowhawk • *Accipiter nisus*

28-34cm, 11–13in

When Throughout the year **Where** Woodland, open countryside and hedgerows **Confusion species** Goshawk **Call** At nest site repeats *kyi-kyi-kyi*

◀ In flight, quick bursts of rapid wing beats interspersed with short glides. Note the distinctive wing shape, quite unlike Goshawk. When soaring, they look flat-winged and the tail is only occasionally fanned.

◀ **Juveniles** are brown above and coarsely barred below. Brownish-looking upperparts are neatly scalloped by broad pale fringes to main feather tracts. Head is brown, flecked white. Barring on underparts is brown and broader than adults.

▲ **Males'** upper-parts are wholly blue-grey with dark wingtips. Underparts are finely-barred orange-red from throat to belly.

▶ **Females** larger than **males** (above) but both sexes share broad, blunted short wings, a small-headed look and a long square-ended tail.

◀ **Females** have dark grey-brown upperparts except for a white supercilium and blackish-looking bars on the tail. Underparts show a white base colour and fine, grey, horizontal barring from the upper breast to the belly.

◀ Prey is usually taken to a regular 'plucking' spot, which is either on the ground, or on a post or tree stump.

Goshawk • *Accipiter gentilis*

49-56cm, 19.5–22in

When Present all year, best in early spring **Where** Large woodland areas, mixed or coniferous, mainly in northern Britain **Confusion species** Sparrowhawk **Call** A deep, fierce-sounding *keeya-keeya-keeya*

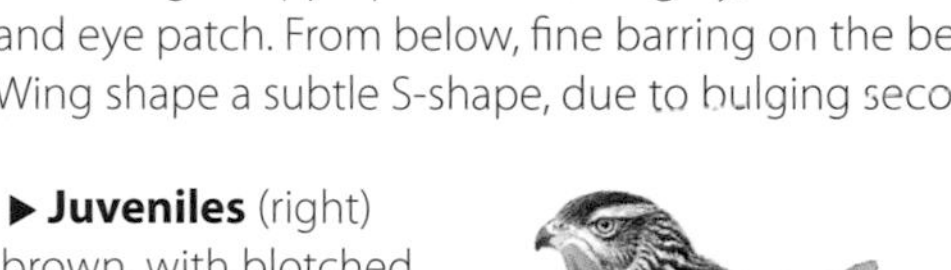

▶ In flight broad, long wings, broad tails, more rounded at the edges. Upperparts are steel-grey, with darker cap and eye patch. From below, fine barring on the belly. Wing shape a subtle S-shape, due to bulging secondaries.

▶ **Juveniles** (right) brown, with blotched white upperparts. Underparts pale buff- yellow, with bold 'teardrop' markings.

▶ **Adult** (far right) Note the barred uppertail, and fine dark barring on the white underparts.

A medium-large, shy raptor, far rarer than the smaller Sparrowhawk. Males larger than female Sparrowhawk, big females are as large as Common Buzzards. Marked size difference between males and females.

Common Buzzard • *Buteo buteo*

46-58cm, 18–22.5in

When Throughout the year. Passage birds in spring and autumn **Where** Around much of the country, favouring mixed woodland near farmland, also moorland and heaths **Confusion species** Rough-legged and Honey Buzzard, Osprey **Call** A cat-like *mee-uuw*

▼ A characteristic, broad-winged bird of prey with a number of different plumage variations. Pale underparts, with slight brown flecking on the breast sides (inviting confusion with Rough-legged Buzzard for the unwary).

▲ In flight, particularly when gliding, the wing profile is distinctive. Wings always held slightly above body level, with wing tips slightly upturned.

▲ Broad wings, large head and shortish tail are easily seen when soaring overhead. From above, Buzzards show little contrast, a paler rump and covert bar may be seen.

Rough-legged Buzzard • *Buteo lagopus*

49–59cm, 23in

When Mainly in late autumn and winter **Where** Coastal grazing marshes, open fields. Primarily east coast **Confusion species** Common Buzzard **Call** Silent in winter

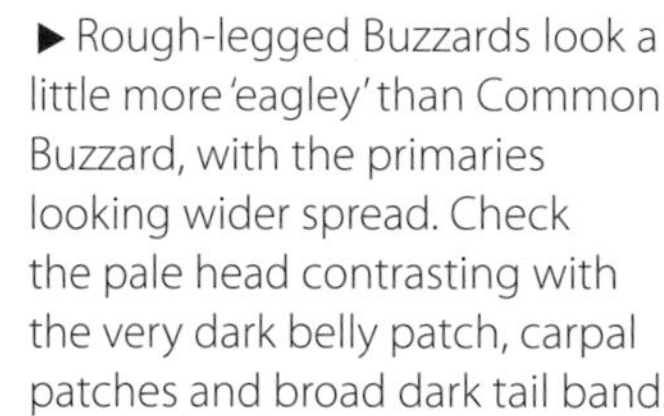

◀ From above, the upper-parts look greyer-brown, with the broad tail band, contrasting with white remainder.

▶ Rough-legged Buzzards look a little more 'eagley' than Common Buzzard, with the primaries looking wider spread. Check the pale head contrasting with the very dark belly patch, carpal patches and broad dark tail band.

◀ Looks slightly larger and longer-winged than Common Buzzard; be careful when separating the two. 'Rough-legs' are more prone to hover and have a generally slower flight.

▼ The generally pale appearance becomes more obvious when they are perched or sitting on the ground, particularly on a **juvenile.** Note the rather oatmeal-toned head, contrasting with the medium-brown upperparts. The pale head markings extend down onto the breast, which, in turn, contrast with the dark belly patch.

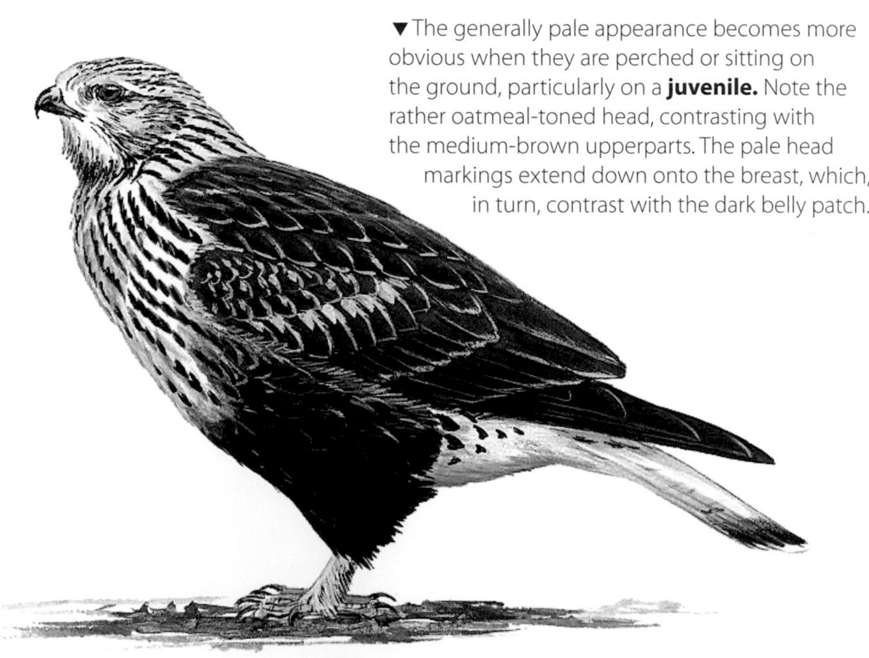

Osprey • *Pandion haliaetus*

52-60cm, 20-23in

When Arrives from early spring onwards, leaves in mid-autumn **Where** Scottish pine forests near water. Many re-introduced birds in England **Confusion species** Common Buzzard **Call** Thin whistling *kew, kew, kew*

Ospreys are slimmer and longer-winged than Common Buzzard, with very distinctive brown and white plumage. Around 100 pairs breed in Scotland every year and, recently, a wild pair reared young in England for the first time in over 150 years.

▼ As they drift along, the wings appear slightly bowed, with the wing tips slightly upturned.

▲ The bow-winged look is also seen after an Osprey has caught a fish.

▲ When hunting, Ospreys will hover frequently, the wing beats looking heavy and laboured. Will dive feet first into the water.

◀ Ospreys have entirely brown upperparts and white underparts, with variable streaking across the breast.

Golden Eagle • *Aquila chrysaetos*

80-93cm, 36in

When Throughout the year **Where** Confined mostly to the hilly areas of the Scottish Highlands and Western Isles, reintroduced to Ireland **Confusion species** Common Buzzard,White-tailed Eagle **Call** Mainly silent

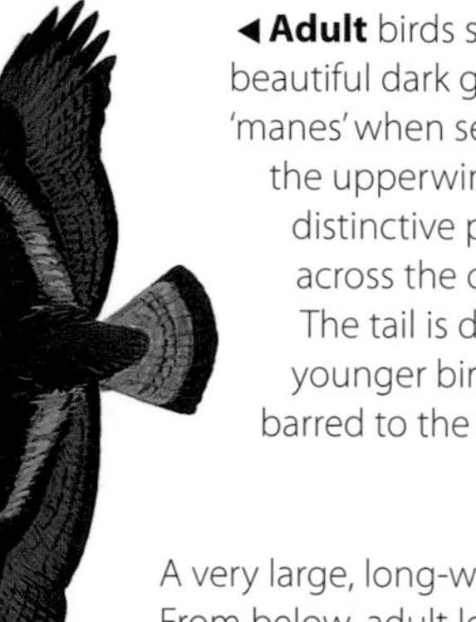

◀ **Adult** birds show beautiful dark golden 'manes' when seen well, and the upperwing shows distinctive pale patches across the coverts. The tail is darker than younger birds, and barred to the tail band.

▼ This **sub-adult** shows the distinctive shape of the species. Note bulging secondaries and longish tail, complete with dark tail band. Underwing shows dirty-white patches. Whiter and cleaner on adults.

A very large, long-winged, long-tailed bird. From below, adult looks rather dark. There is some contrast on the underwing and undertail - but lacks the pale patches of younger birds.

Common Kestrel • *Falco tinnunculus*

31-37cm, 14in

When Year round **Where** Anywhere, from cities to upland moors **Confusion species** Hobby **Call** A loud, harsh, repeated *kee-kee-kee-kee*

In flight, **female** (left), **male** (right and below).

▼ **Females** (right) larger than males, streaked warm-brown above and buff below. Rufous mantle has dark bars extending to the wing coverts. Barred rump greyer-brown. Tail shows six to seven dark bars.

Easily told from other raptors by their size, longish tail and noticeably pointed wings.

▶ **Males** (left) have a blue-grey head, dark moustache and buff throat. Mantle and wing coverts are chestnut with black spotting and barring. Broad black tail bar on grey tail.

Merlin • *Falco columbarius*

26-33cm, 13in

When Throughout the year. More frequent in autumn and winter **Where** Breeds on northern open moorland and heath. Winters around coasts, also at raptor roosts **Confusion species** Kestrel, Hobby **Call** Silent, except at nest. Alarm call a repeated *kikikikikiki*

Our smallest falcon, with distinctive structural and plumage features. Can be rather elusive,

▶ A 'whippy rapid wingbeat. Incredibly agile, twisting and turning as they keep up with prey. From below, note the streaked breast and underwing.

◀ **Adult males** (far right) are bluish above, with a dark trailing edge. An orange tint to the collar may be seen, also a bluish cast to the head and a hint of a moustachial stripe. **Females** (left) are brown above, with pale face and no moustachial stripes. Underparts off-white with bold brown streaks.

Hobby • *Falco subbuteo*

29-35 cm, 14 in

When Arrives from mid-April onwards, leaves mid-autumn **Where** Nests in woodland and around heathland, mainly in southern Britain. Passage birds more widespread **Confusion species** Kestrel, Merlin **Call** Similar to other small falcons, a high pitched tew-tew-tew.Also both sexes have a sharp *kic-chit* note given in flight

▶ Aerial feeders, hunting insects and small birds. Very acrobatic birds. When feeding young, adults will range several miles in search of food.

▶ **Adults** Head has black cap. Dark blue-grey upper- parts, with darker wings and tail. Streaked underparts and underwings. Tail barred with red undertail. Note the obvious red 'trousers'.

Similar in size to Kestrel, but has longer more pointed wings and squarer tail. Also quicker and more agile.

◀ **Juveniles** lack any red on the undertail.

Peregrine • *Falco peregrinus*

38-45cm, 18in

When Year round **Where** Cliffs of western Britain and Ireland, also mountains and quarries. Increasingly found in cities too. Winters away from breeding areas **Confusion species** Hobby, Kestrel **Call** A piercing, harsh *reek-reek-reek-reek*

Chunky, large falcons with pointed wings, broad tail and barrel-chest. As with some other birds of prey, there is a difference in the size of the sexes, females larger than males.

▲ From below, the blackish-looking cap is prominent as are the barred underparts. Peregrines lack the agility of smaller falcons, but make up for it in power.

▼ Often before stooping at 100mph plus, Peregrines will soar, like this **juvenile** (below), in 'the cross of death'!

▲ **Adult** (above) when seen perched, note the cap, bold yellow eye ring, dark moustachials, slate blue upperparts, along with black bars and 'arrowheads' on the underparts.

▶ **Juveniles** (right) are browner and streakier than adults. The head pattern is brown and less pronounced. The upperparts are also browner, while the underparts show bold 'teardrops'.

Water Rail • *Rallus aquaticus*

23-26cm, 9-10in

When Throughout the year, autumn and winter best **Where** Marshes and reedbeds, but also damp thickets and wet woodland across much of country **Confusion species** Spotted Crake **Call** Wide range of calls, but its 'squealing pig' call is most common (descends quickly) or a sharp *pip* contact call

A fairly small, podgy, very shy and secretive bird. Probably more common than we realise, birds are known to arrive from the continent in the autumn.

▶ **Adults** have obvious blue-grey faces and underparts, barred flanks, and buff-white undertail. Bill is redder than the juvenile's with a dark culmen.

◀ **Juveniles,** paler on head and underparts than adults. Creamy supercilium and white throat. Upperparts tawny-brown, with bold, black streaks on the mantle and upperwing.

Spotted Crake • *Porzana porzana*

19-22.5cm, 7.5-8.5in

When Occasionally in spring, mainly in late summer to early autumn. Rare breeding bird **Where** Breeding birds favour sedge bogs rather than reedbeds. Passage birds on freshwater marshes anywhere **Confusion species** Water Rail **Call** Distinctive song, heard at breeding sites, like a whistle or cracking whip *hew-itt, hew-itt*

▶ A very spotty bird! Particularly spring adults, but any autumn bird will have white spots on its neck and upper- parts. Flanks are finely striped black and white and they have buff undertails. The bill is short and straight, often yellowish. Juveniles look duller all over.

◀ Resembles a short-billed, small Water Rail and shares similar habitat, especially in the autumn. Often very secretive, but can appear on the edge of reedbeds, particularly in autumn.

Moorhen • *Gallinula chloropus*

27-31 cm, 11 in

When Throughout the year **Where** Ornamental lakes, ponds, rivers and marshes across the country **Confusion species** Coot, Water Rail (juvenile only) **Call** Explosive *kee-rrl* or sharp *kik-keek*

A distinctive medium-sized waterbird, with a round head and body, as well as short wings. On land, Moorhens appear to be ungainly and timid. Yellowy-green legs and large feet are obvious.

◀ **Juveniles** show none of the adult's colour. Head is dark brown with a greyish wash on the face. Chin and throat are white, while the remainder of the underparts are grey-brown.

▼ **Adults'** head and underparts are a dark greyish-blue, with browner upperparts. Along the flank is an obvious white line, which appears very bold against the dark wing and body feathers. The rear end is blackish, except for a gleaming white undertail. The frontal shield and bill (except for the yellow tip) are cherry-red, as is the eye.

Coot • *Fulica atra*

36-42cm, 14-16in

When Throughout the year **Where** Lakes, rivers, marshes, reservoirs and gravel pits around the country (except northern Scotland) **Confusion species** Moorhen **Call** Low coot, as well as an abrupt *kek*

▲ Flocks of Coot gather in open water (unlike Moorhens).They dive into deeper water to feed. Reservoirs in some areas of Britain host massive winter flocks of Coot.

▼ **Juveniles** (top) lack the white frontal shield, and have ashy- grey upperparts, contrasting with the white throat and breast. The flanks are ashy grey. The bill is silvery-grey.

Plump-bodied birds, with small heads and short tails, similar in shape to Moorhen, but clearly larger.

▶ **Adults** (bottom) are dark ashy-grey all over (darkest on the head), with white bill and frontal shield. The legs are grey. When out of the water, note their amazing lobbed feet!

Corncrake • *Crex crex*

22-25cm, 9-9.5in

When Arrive from early May onwards. Passage birds almost always in autumn **Where** Breeds widely in Ireland, and also Western Isles, in damp meadows. Passage birds coastal **Confusion species** Young gamebirds **Call** Plaintive, echoing *earph-earph,* heard almost non-stop in breeding season

▶ Slimmer than partridges, resembling Water Rail in shape. Plumage is mainly warm-brown, except for the grey face and breast, along with a ginger patch on the wings.

▲ If lucky, you may see one emerging from cover and begin to sing. The **male** will tilt his head back and begin to call.

One of the most enigmatic birds seen in Britain. Highly secretive and very rare, this smallish bird (half the size of a Grey Partridge) has begun to make a comeback in recent years. Looking very round-winged in flight; Corncrakes dangle their legs before landing.

Common Crane • *Grus grus*

96-119cm, 38–46in

When Year round. Migrants mainly autumn, some in winter **Where** Norfolk Broads throughout the year, also Cambridgeshire fenland. Otherwise mainly coastal, but can appear anywhere. Very rare breeding species **Confusion species** Grey Heron, White Stork **Call** Most commonly heard is deep, far carrying *krrow* or *kraaw*

Huge birds, standing very tall. Broad wings, long necks and legs. An atypical, largely sedentary, tiny population exists in Norfolk, where up to three pairs breed.

◀ **Adults are** unmistakable. The head shows a neat red 'skull cap', contrasting with the black and white head and neck. The mantle is washed brown and the grey wings often show black and brown feather centres. Note the immense 'bushy' grey and black tail.

◀ The bill is straw-yellow and the long legs grey.

▲ In flight, looks very large with neck and legs extended. Strongly contrasting wing pattern.

▶ **Juvenile** shows a gingery head and neck with the remainder of the plumage soft grey, with varying degrees of ginger feather- centres on the wings and mantle.

Stone Curlew • *Burhinus oedicnemus*

38–45cm, 17.5in

When Arrives early to mid-March. Passage birds into early summer, also in autumn **Where** Breeds mainly in East Anglia on sandy heathland and arable land. Also in southern England **Confusion species** None **Call** Display call, a wailing, sad-sounding *kurrr-lee* repeated often

▼Great camouflage plumage, pale fawns, browns and white helps them blend in with their surroundings. Head pattern, black-tipped bill, long yellow legs and upperwing pattern are very distinctive; as is the yellow eye. Both sexes share the incubation of the eggs and youngsters and are often very tricky to see when on the nest.

▶ Reminiscent of a large out-sized pale brown plover, with long legs and fairly chunky bill. Habitually walks or runs rather than flying.

Oystercatcher • *Haematopus ostralegus*

39-44cm, 17in

When Throughout the year, migrants in winter **Where** Found around entire coastline, also increasingly common sight inland **Confusion species** None **Call** A noisy, excitable *kleep-kleep-kleep*

▶ Easily identified in flight. Black upperparts are interrupted by a broad white wing bar and white rump, extending well up the back. Sexes are identical, with glossy black upperparts (white on wings) and white underparts. Long orange-red bill often has a paler tip. Thick pink legs. Red eye, with orange orbital ring.

▶ In **winter** (far right) look a little less glossy and show a white neck collar.

A common, distinctive large wader seen throughout the year around Britain and Ireland. During the early autumn and into the winter, Oystercatchers from Scandinavia and Iceland journey to Britain and join large communal flocks.

Avocet • *Recurvirostra avosetta*

42-46cm, 16.5–18in

When Throughout the year **Where** Breeds on shallow lagoons, mainly in East Anglia. Winters on estuaries in east and south-west **Confusion species** None **Call** Ringing *klup-klup-klup*

A large, instantly recognizable wader, representing one of the great conservation stories of the 20th century. Returning as a breeding species to East Anglia after World War II, careful site management has seen populations soar.

◄ In flight, note the pied plumage, upturned bill and feet trailing behind the white tail.

▼ **Adults** are beautiful, elegant birds. The glossy black of the head, nape and wings contrasts with the dazzling white remainder of the plumage. The slender, upturned bill always looks amazing! The long legs are dull-blue.

▲ **Juveniles** have dingy upperpart markings, brownish rather than black, and the white appears duller and more sullied.

Lapwing • *Vanellus vanellus*

28-31cm, 12in

When Throughout the year **Where** Breeds on arable farmland and damp marshes. Winter birds on estuaries too **Confusion species** None **Call** A shrill *peeee-wich,* which led to the alternate name of Peewit

▲ This roosting autumn group show round bodies and small, crested heads. Medium-sized, stocky birds, with a unique appearance. They move widely around the country in hard winters.

▶ Rounded wings in flight. On warmer, late winter days, male Lapwings begin to display, flying in amazing tumbles, calling frequently and loudly to attract a female.

▶ **Breeding** birds have a long black crest that wafts around in a breeze. Face and breast are black (paler on females), contrasting with the white face and white underparts. Upperparts are green, with startling purple iridescence.

Golden Plover • *Pluvialis apricaria*

25-28cm, 11in

When Year round **Where** Breeds on uplands and moors. In winter on farmland, coastal marshes and estuaries **Confusion species** Dotterel, Grey Plover **Call** A mournful *flu-ee*

Medium-sized waders, with small heads, slim bills, roundish bodies and longish legs.

▶ **Juveniles and adults** show striking white under-wing. Notice long-wings.

▲ **Non breeding** birds are plain-faced, with golden notches on upperparts. Underparts streaked on breast, note gold and black-barred tail. Tail falls short of the longest primary.

◀ **Breeding** birds have black upperparts with golden spangles on every feather. White band on nead, extending to breast and flanks. Face black on 'Northern' birds, 'Southern' birds have more mottled look. Both have black bellies and white undertails.

Grey Plover • *Pluvialis squatarola*

26-29cm, 11 in

When Can be found year round, almost resident **Where** Found around coasts on estuaries, mudflats and inland on muddy lakes **Confusion species** Golden Plover **Call** Similar to Golden Plover, a sad sounding *peee-oo-eee*

◀ In flight, **juveniles** show diagnostic black axillaries ('armpit'). They look larger in flight than Golden Plover.

Fairly chunky birds, looking distinctly heavier than Golden Plover, with a more pot-bellied look, a larger head and a heavier bill.

▶ **Breeding** birds have very silver and white looking plumage. The broad white band from the lores to the flank catches the eye as it contrasts strongly with the black face and belly patch. Upperparts are black with bold silver fringes and edges.

◀ **Non breeding** birds look fairly dull compared to their immaculate summer dress. Upperparts look entirely grey-brown. Underparts are greyish on breast with paler flanks and undertail.

Little Ringed Plover • *Charadrius dubius*

15.5-18cm, 7in

When Arrives from mid-March onwards, leaving by October **Where** Nests on bare sandy or gravel areas alongside fresh water, mainly south-east England. Migrants on coastal marshes **Confusion species** Ringed and Kentish Plover **Call** A loud, high-pitched *pee-you*

▶ **Adults** (top) have distinctive head pattern - narrow black bands on head and breast. Upperparts paler brown than Ringed Plover; note tapering rear end. Bright yellow eye ring (absent on Ringed) and fine, black, thorn-like bill. Legs and feet are pinkish-yellow.

▶ **Juveniles** (right) are fairly plain faced, except for a small pale area on the lores. Upperparts look scaly in appearance, while the breast band is fairly diffuse.

▲ In flight, appear slim and long winged. Upperwing clearly shows no wingbar.

Ringed Plover • *Charadrius hiaticula*

17-19.5cm, 6in

When Throughout the year. Passage birds in spring and autumn **Where** Sand or shingle beaches, tidal estuaries and mudflats around all coasts **Confusion species** Little Ringed and Kentish Plover **Call** A soft *too-lee*

▶ **Adults** have broad black bands around head and breast, dark brown above. Thick, stubby bill is orange with black tip, legs are orange; yellow eye ring absent.

▶ **Juveniles** (right) differ from juvenile Little Ringed - whitish forehead and supercilium, unlike plain Little Ringed. Upperparts are darker brown. Blackish bill, with a pale base.

Slightly larger and stockier than Little Ringed Plover. Dumpier, larger head, shorter looking rear end and heavier bill. Small, dark Ringed Plovers in spring may be Tundra' birds. Non breeding birds look dull. Upperparts entirely grey-brown. Underparts greyish on breast with paler flanks and undertail.

Kentish Plover • *Charadrius alexandrinus* 15-17cm, 7in

When Appears in early spring onwards. Occasionally in autumn, very rare winter bird **Where** Coastal marshes, estuaries and beaches **Confusion species** Ringed and Little Ringed Plover **Call** Rarely heard, a dry *trrrrip*

In flight, Kentish Plover shows a narrow white wingbar (not as broad as Ringed Plover, but far more obvious than on Little Ringed Plover) and white tail sides.

◀ **Adults** have almost chick-like look. **Male** (bottom) shows rufous rear-crown, with black fore-crown and small black breast sides, also a distinctive, narrow, black eyestripe, features that are all lacking in the **female** (top).

◀ Both sexes are cold ashy-grey brown above and white below, also share the rather thin black bill (reminiscent of Little Ringed Plover) and black legs.

◀ Quite small, long-legged and thinner-billed birds than Ringed Plover, stockier and less attenuated than Little Ringed.

Dotterel • *Charadrius morinellus* 20.5-24cm, 9in

When Arrives from late April onwards. Autumn birds leave by October **Where** Breeds on Scottish mountains. Passage birds almost anywhere, favour traditional sites **Confusion species** Golden Plover **Call** Soft sounding *pyurr*

▶ In flight, shows silvery- grey underwing.

▼ **Juveniles** more common in autumn than adults. Dark crowns, with white supercilium. Upperparts dark, with pale edges.

Smaller, more rounded than Golden Plover, with smaller bill. Spring Dotterels have a habit of turning up in small groups ('trips'), usually on upland areas or wheat and pea fields.

◀ **Adults.** Females brighter than males. Dark crown contrasts strongly with white supercilium and throat. Upper breast is greyish with white (edged black) breast band. Lower breast and belly are rufous.

Black-tailed Godwit • *Limosa limosa*

37-42cm, 16in

When On spring and autumn passage. Also wintering species **Where** Rare breeding species in wet meadows. Elsewhere favours coastal marshes, estuaries and mudflats **Confusion species** Bar-tailed Godwit **Call** Silent in flying flocks. Feeding birds chatter to each other. Display call *reeta-reetc-reeta-keehit-keehit*

► **Juveniles'** plumage immaculate. Not as colourful as adults, but still richly coloured.

► **Breeding** plumage (middle), upperparts boldly marked with reds, blacks and greys contrasting with the 'tomato soup' coloured underparts. Birds from Iceland ***(islandica)*** are deeper red below with shorter bill and legs. 'Our' birds – ***(limosa)*** are greyer above and more orange below.

► In flight**, winter adult** has broad white upperwing bar and black tail shared by all ages.

◄ Non breeding almost wholly silvery-grey above with grey breast and flanks and white underparts.

Bar-tailed Godwit • *Limosa lapponica*

33-41 cm, 15in

When In spring and autumn, but predominantly a winter species **Where** Tidal flats and estuaries. Sandy beaches **Confusion species** Black-tailed Godwit **Call** Often heard in flight, a *seewee-seewee* repeated note

A medium-sized wader with longish slightly upturned bill and longish legs.

► In flight, differences between Bar- and Black-tailed are clear. Upperwing lacks broad wing bars and tail is finely barred. Toes just visible beyond tail.

► **Non breeding** birds told from Black-tailed cousins by more marked upperparts, dumpier overall look, upturned bill and shorter leg length.

◄ **Juveniles** (middle) although neat, lack elegance of Black-tailed Godwit. Upperparts look 'scored' like the adults, but more variegated.

◄ **Adult** breeding, underparts are brick red, contrasting with neat ginger and black upperparts and greyish wings.

Whimbrel • *Numenius phaeopus*

37-45cm, 17in

When On passage in spring and autumn. Occasionally in winter. Some summer **Where** Breeds on Scottish moorland and bogs. Passage birds seen on coastal meadows, occasionally inland **Confusion species** Curlew **Call** Passage birds give a distinctive, high-pitched *whu-whu-whu-whu-whu-whu-whu.* Affectionately known as the 'Seven Whistler'

A smaller, neater version of the Curlew, with a smaller decurved bill and striking head pattern.

▲ In flight, Whimbrels resemble Curlews (and even Bar-tailed Godwits), but good views should show the shorter decurved bill and slightly darker upperwing. Often vocal, especially on migration.

▼ When seen feeding, the darker upperparts are fairly obvious. Most prominent feature is the head pattern, quite unlike the plain-headed look of the larger Curlew (beware though - early autumn birds can look very worn on the head and not very stripy). The shorter, bluer legs are also to be looked for. Again, notice the bill length and shape.

Curlew • *Numenius arquata*

48-57cm, 23in

When Passage birds in spring and autumn. Widespread in winter too **Where** Breeds on moorland and damp, rough grassland. Passage/winter birds on coastal marshes, saltings, estuaries and farmland **Confusion species** Whimbrel **Call** Frequently heard in flight or on the ground, a ringing *kerr-leew*. Song is a lovely descending, liquid set of notes

A large brownish wader with a long down-curved bill and uniform plumage.

▶ Sometimes tricky to separate Curlew from Whimbrel in flight, look for a long bill (beware some male Curlews have small bills), whiter underwing and more contrasting upperwing. Curlew flocks often fly in a 'V' formation when migrating.

▼ There should be little trouble separating Curlew from Whimbrel on the ground. The head markings are very uniform brown on Curlew (lacking the bold stripes of Whimbrel) and the upperparts are a little warmer-toned than Whimbrel. There is a fawn wash to the breast and upper flanks on Curlew (greyer on Whimbrel) and the streaks are bolder on Curlew. But most obvious of all - the bill...it's so long! Some bills look larger than this bird's.

Ruff • *Philomachus pugnax*

29-32cm, 12in

When Few over-winter, many arrive from April onwards. Autumn passage from mid- July onwards **Where** Rare breeding species in wet meadows. Passage/winter birds on freshwater marshes, estuaries, reservoirs and fields **Confusion species** Dunlin, Redshank, Wood and Buff-breasted Sandpiper (autumn only) **Call** Very rarely heard. Occasional low grunts

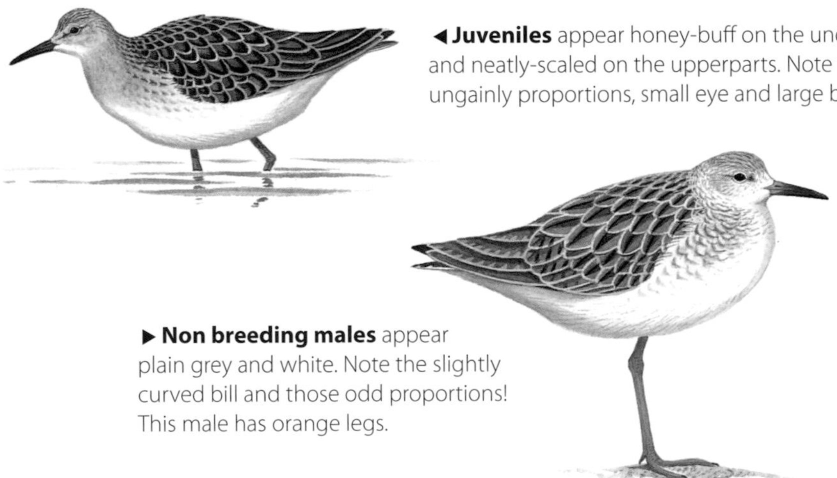

◀ **Juveniles** appear honey-buff on the underparts and neatly-scaled on the upperparts. Note the ungainly proportions, small eye and large bill.

▶ **Non breeding males** appear plain grey and white. Note the slightly curved bill and those odd proportions! This male has orange legs.

▼ Medium-sized waders, note the differences between the two sexes. Both share characteristic small head, pot belly and longish legs. In flight, Ruff have a thin wing bar and white 'horse shoe' rumps.

▼ **Females** (centre) look smaller and dowdy in comparison - almost scaled around the head and neck.

◀ **Breeding males** (left) in spring can come in any sort of spectacular dress. The darker-ruffed birds are always more dominant at leks.

Turnstone • *Arenaria interpres*

21-24cm, 10in

When Mainly a winter visitor, seen on spring and autumn passage. Some summer **Where** Rocky coastlines and shingle beaches around Britain **Confusion species** None **Call** A scratchy, chattering *kut-kut-a-kut*

Stocky, short- legged, medium- sized wader with distinctive habits.

▲ **Non breeding** bird appears pied, although some brown may be apparent on the upperparts. Face is mottled-grey with black breast and white underparts.

▼ **Juveniles** resemble winter adults, except for paler gingery fringing on upperparts.

▲ **Breeding** birds show a white and black patterned face with rich colourful patterning on the upperparts. Also several intermediate plumages, combining summer and winter feathers.

Curlew Sandpiper • *Calidris ferruginea*

19-21.5cm, 8in

When Mid- to late spring, late summer and autumn **Where** Freshwater marshes (often coastal), inland reservoirs and lakes **Confusion species** Dunlin **Call** Ringing, pleasing *cherr-upp*

▶ **Non breeding** birds (left) silvery- grey, with a pale \ face, compared to the moulting adult (right).

Elegant waders, slightly larger than Dunlin, with a longer, more decurved bill and an obvious white rump in flight.

▶ **Juveniles** (back) can appear in large numbers at some sites during the autumn. Upperparts are beautifully fresh and scaly-looking, while the breast shows a warm apricot wash.

▶ **Breeding adults** (front) seen at the end of spring or start of autumn. The brick-red underparts can appear very intense in colour.

Knot • *Calidris canutus*

23-26cm, 8.5in

When Mainly in late summer into winter. Some in spring **Where** Large numbers restricted to mudflats of east coast, Ireland and Scotland **Confusion species** None **Call** Rarely heard; a soft *khet-khet*

Plump, squat-looking waders, with a shortish bill and short legs. In the autumn and winter, flocks of tens of thousands of these birds can be seen in areas such as the Wash. Some birds may show variable amounts of red breeding plumage.

▲**Juveniles** seen in autumn only, are very neat-looking birds - the upperparts are entirely grey with narrow black chevrons on the individual feathers, which look almost neat. The breast is washed buff, with fine dark streaking.

▲**Breeding** (seen in autumn too) are brick-red below, with black wings, edged and notched with white and rufous. The short, straight bill is black and the legs vary from green to black.

▼**Non breeding** birds look entirely plain grey above and whitish below. In flight, they show a pale rump.

Sanderling • *Calidris alba*

18-21 cm, 8in

When Arrive here from September onwards. Some in spring and summer **Where** Around all coasts, especially on sandy beaches. Sometimes on marshes **Confusion species** Dunlin, Little Stint **Call** A strident *piip*

Similar in size to Dunlin, but appear more compact, with shorter bills and legs. Larger than Little Stint.

▲ Non breeding adults are almost entirely pale silver-grey on the upperparts, with darker feather centres and dark primaries. Underparts show grey 'thumbprints' on the breast sides.The stout looking bill is black, as are the legs, which often look clockwork, given the speed they run. Often seen in small flocks on beaches chasing the edge of the sea.

◀ **Juveniles** resemble a non breeding bird, but are more heavily demarcated on the upperparts. Underparts show a yellow wash to the streaky thumb marks on the breast.

▶ **Breeding** adults show warm-brown tones to the upperparts. A brown full breast band is often seen, and sometimes the 'face' can look quite orangey. Partial summer plumage also occurs from late spring to early autumn.

Little Stint • *Calidris minuta*

14-15.5cm, 6in

When Relatively common passage migrant. Scarce in spring, more common in autumn **Where** Mud-fringed pools, lakes and reservoir edges, coastal mudflats **Confusion species** Temminck's Stint, Dunlin, Sanderling **Call** Sharp, repeated *piip*

Smaller than Dunlin, with fine, short bill, and quick, busy feeding actions, always pecking at the mud.

◀ **Breeding** birds have indistinct, creamy braces on the mantle. Note the split supercilium. Bill is fine-tipped and black, usually fairly short. Plumage is gingery, with black feather centres.

▶ **Adult winter** birds appear wholly grey, and only stragglers (from November onwards) appear like this. Similar plumage to Sanderling, but note the differences in size, structure and feeding action.

◀ **Juveniles** can be very variable. Head shows a pale forehead and split supercilium contrasting with a dark crown and nape. Mantle shows distinctive white braces. The breast sides are dark buff with fine streaks.

Temminck's Stint • *Calidris temminckii*

13.5-15cm, 5.5in

When Mid-May to mid-June, occasionally in August and September **Where** Coastal marshes (especially on east coast), inland reservoirs and pools. Very rare breeder in Scotland **Confusion species** Little Stint **Call** Loud, trilling *tirrr-tirrr-tirrr*

▶ **Breeding** adults lack the gingery tones of Little Stint. Grey-brown upperparts with large black feather centres. Notice slightly decurved bill and breast band.

◀ Autumn birds are rare and are invariably **juveniles**. They lack the white braces of Little Stint and appear greyer-brown and more scaled. Legs are dirty-yellow, typical of the species.

▶ **Non breeding adults** appear almost wholly-grey, although this plumage is rarely seen here. Notice remnant summer feathers on the scapulars.

Dunlin • *Calidris alpina*

17-21 cm, 8in

When Wintering species and passage migrant in spring and autumn **Where** Breeds on high moorlands. Widespread around coastline, marshes, lagoons **Confusion species** Curlew Sandpiper, Little Stint, rarer waders **Call** A trilled *kreeit* in flight

▼ **Winter** birds eventually moult into wholly grey and white plumage. Stocky and compact, decurved black bills and shortish legs. Bill size and length varies.

◀ **Juveniles** lack the distinctive black belly patch of a breeding adult. Shares white mantle braces with Little Stint, but size difference always apparent.

▶ A widespread common wader, with a variety of plumages that need to be learnt carefully! **Breeding** plumaged birds look pretty smart! Rufous-tinged crown and mantle with the familiar black belly. Some birds can look very frosty on the upperparts, others duller.

Purple Sandpiper • *Calidris maritima* 19-22cm, 8.5in

When Arrives from early September onwards, leaving early spring **Where** Almost exclusively rocky coastlines, particularly in south-west England, Scotland and Ireland. Very rare breeding species **Confusion species** Dunlin **Call** Generally heard when disturbed or in flight, a hard *quiit*

◀ **Juveniles** (top) show three neat rows of ginger-fringed scapulars, contrasting with the remainder of the upperwing. Note fine streaks on flanks, characteristic of all ages of Purple Sandpiper.

◀ **Non breeding** adults (middle) not particularly purple, more a delicate smooth blue-grey above, and whitish below. Note distinctive spot on lores and slightly decurved short, orange-based bill.

◀ **Adults** in breeding plumage (bottom) darker than winter birds, with rufous crown and notches on upperwing.

Buff-breasted Sandpiper • *Tryngites subruficollis* 19cm, 7.5in

When Mainly autumn, but occasionally in spring/summer **Where** Likes short-turf areas (airfields particularly) and marshes. Mostly south-west England and Ireland **Confusion species** Ruff **Call** Rarely heard, but do utter a soft, low *gurrf*

◀ **Juveniles** (left) resemble **Ruff** Face plain, except for head markings and large-looking black eyes. Rest of face and under-pays are honey-buff, fading to whitish on the belly and undertail. Note finely-spotted breast sides. Upperparts finely scalloped black, with fine, pale fringes. Crucially, they have a long primary projection and long tertials cloak the primaries. Delicate proportions, compared to Ruff. Always appear round-headed with a portly belly and smaller bill.

▼ **Adults,** richer in tone on the underparts but are, invariably, rather more scruffy on the upperparts. In flight, looks like a small plover. Check the underwing pattern - they have an obvious dark crescent on the pale underwing.

Pectoral Sandpiper • *Calidris melanotos* 19-23cm, 8-9in

When Occasionally in spring and summer, mostly in autumn **Where** Coastal freshwater marshes, lagoons, pools and inland reservoirs. Both east and west coasts **Confusion species** Dunlin **Call** Dry, trilling *krrrp*

Our most common North American vagrant. Also breed in north-east Siberia, and it is likely we get them from there as well. Juveniles are fresher-loo king, with brighter, rufous tones. The shortish bill has a pale base, note the greenish-yellow legs.

▶ Larger than Dunlin, with a pot-bellied look, and shorter decurved bill. The head appears capped, but the most obvious feature is the sharply demarcated pectoral breast band. The upperparts are dark brown.

▲ In flight, look rather stout and a little pot bellied. Dark on the upperparts, with only an indistinct wingbar visible. The sides of the rump are noticeably white darker towards the tail.

Common Sandpiper • *Actitis hypoleucos* *18.5-20cm, 7.5in*

When Summer migrant, arriving from April onwards. Autumn passage begins in July **Where** Breeds along stony river shores, sometimes seashore. Found around pools, lakes and reservoirs on passage **Confusion species** Green and Wood Sandpiper **Call** Clear, piping rapid *swee-swee swee-swee*

A medium-sized wader, with horizontal gait and distinctive behaviour.

▶ **Juveniles** (top) adapt well from upland streams and rivers to autumn stop-off points. More scaly on the upperparts compared to adults, with barred coverts.

▶ **Breeding** birds are covered in fine, black streaks on the upperparts. Notice constant bobbing of its longish tail as it feeds.

▲ In flight, the wings barely come above body level and are noticeably bowed. Slim, white wing bar and dark-looking, barred tail.

Green Sandpiper • *Tringa ochropus*

20-24cm, 8–9in

When Mainly in autumn, a few appear in spring. Also winters in southern England **Where** Found in damp bogs, meadows, tidal creeks, inland waters **Confusion species** Wood and Common Sandpiper **Call** Soft *tueee-wit-wit* with repeated *pik*

A bulky-looking wader with a shortish, straight bill, slightly pot-bellied look and shortish legs.

◀ Will announce themselves by flying up in a bit of a tizzy! Black-looking underwing and dark-looking upperwing. Broad, black bars on white tail.

▶ **Juveniles** look blacker than adults, with whiter-looking flecks on upperparts. Both look portly. They bob around in a less busy fashion than the Common Sandpiper.

▲ **Adults** have very dark brown upperparts flecked with pale mottling. The breast has a diffuse band. More pronounced face pattern than the Common Sandpiper.

Wood Sandpiper • *Tringa glareola*

18.5-21 cm, 7.5in

When Spring migrants appear from May onwards. Autumn passage begins July **Where** Breeds (rare) on northern Scottish bogs and marshes. Passage birds on freshwater marshes, muddy-fringed pools **Confusion species** Common and Green Sandpiper **Call** Often heard in flight or when on the ground, an excited *chiff-iff-iff*

A delicate-looking wader, with a smallish head and long legs.

▼ **Juveniles** (top) are similar to adults but always look neater when they arrive in the autumn. Darker brown with more finely notched upperparts.

▲ In flight, less bulky-looking than Green, with narrower wings. Upperwing looks browner, white rump is square. Tail is finely barred, feet project beyond it.

◀ **Adults'** face pattern as juveniles, but can appear darker-capped with a more pronounced supercilium. Upperparts a little greyer. Obvious yellowish legs.

Common Redshank • *Tringa totanus*

24-27cm, 11in

When Throughout the year. Breeding species as well as passage migrant from further afield **Where** Breeds on wet coastal and inland pasture and meadows. Passage/ winter birds also on estuaries, mudflats **Confusion species** Spotted Redshank, Greenshank, Wood Sandpiper, Ruff **Call** A fairly musical *tew-hu-hu*. Song flight a *melodic tooloo-tooloo-tooloo-toolewee*

A medium sized wader with a shortish bill and distinctive plumage at all ages.

▶ In flight, easy to identify. No other British wader shares the white on the trailing edge of the wing and the white extending up the back. Often vocal in flight.

▶ **Non breeding** birds appear fairly cold-grey above, with fine spotting on the wing. Underparts are washed grey on the flanks. Note the white and black narrowish loral patches. Bill reddish at base, legs are red throughout the year.

▲ **Juveniles** resemble a finely barred version of an adult winter, but always looking neater and fresher plumaged. Juveniles can have very orange-looking legs, suggesting other species, such as Ruff.

▶ **Breeding** birds look similar to winter birds, but heavily streaked on upper- and underparts. Bare parts are brighter red too. Look out for the fabulous 'butterfly' display flight in spring.

Spotted Redshank • *Tringa erythropus*

29-33cm, 11–13in

When Mainly in spring, mid-summer and autumn. Also winters in small numbers **Where** Inland or coastal marshes, pools. Winters on estuaries, tidal creeks **Confusion species** Common Redshank, Greenshank **Call** Far-carrying *che-wit*

◀ In flight, note the white V-shape on back. Legs trailing beyond the tail - unlike Common Redshank.

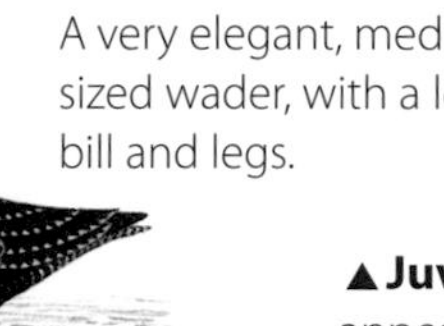

A very elegant, medium-sized wader, with a longish bill and legs.

▲ **Breeding** birds are sooty-black all over with fine white flecks on the upperwing and fine barring on the undertail. Legs blackish in high summer.

▲ **Juveniles** (front) appear from August onwards and look smoky-grey. Finely barred on underparts, neat fringing to upperparts. Legs are bright orange. Note broad white loral mark.

▲ **Non breeding** (back) silvery-grey above with a distinctive face pattern. Red legs.

Greenshank • *Tringa nebularia*

30-34cm, 12-13in

When Spring and autumn passage bird. Winters too **Where** Breeds on northern Scottish moorland and bogs **Confusion species** Common and Spotted Redshank **Call** A loud, ringing *tu-tu-tu.* Song flight is *clue-wee, clue-wee, clue-wee*

◀ In flight, resembles Spotted Redshank, but more white on the upperparts and darker upperwings.

▲ **Juveniles** look almost striped at a distance.

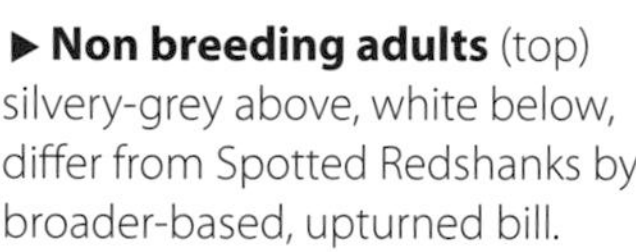

▶ **Non breeding adults** (top) silvery-grey above, white below, differ from Spotted Redshanks by broader-based, upturned bill.

▶ **Breeding adults** darker than winter birds, with bold black feather centres to the upperwing. Head looks a little darker too.

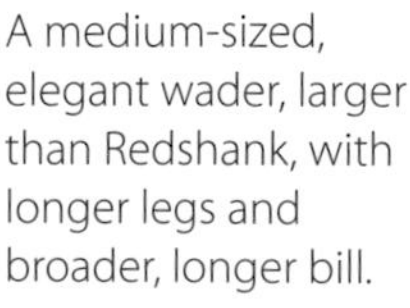

A medium-sized, elegant wader, larger than Redshank, with longer legs and broader, longer bill.

Woodcock • *Scolopax rusticola*

33-38cm, 13-15in

When Throughout the year, spring is best. Autumn migrants too **Where** Breeding birds found in damp woodland (mixed or deciduous). Autumn birds on coast **Confusion species** Snipe **Call** Roding males grunt a *wark-wark-wark-yiup*

▼A medium-sized, very stocky wader, with a long bill and amazing camouflage plumage. Best time to see Woodcock is dawn or dusk on a spring day.They appear over clearings in woodland, in their 'roding' display flight.

▲In flight, the long bill, rounded wings and bright upperwing are obvious. If disturbed, they fly off fairly quickly, low and straight. In less hurried circumstances, they are slower than Snipe. Note the barred underwing and belly.

▼On the ground, the full intricacy of the Woodcock's markings can be appreciated. Note the heavy barring on the crown and the contrasting rufous upperparts and barred buff underparts.

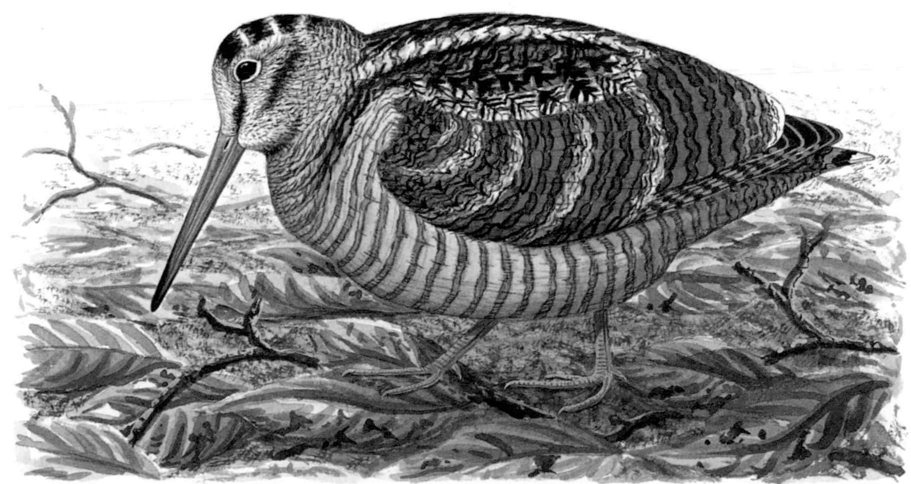

Common Snipe • *Gallinago gallinago*

23-28cm, 9-11 in

When Year round. Passage migrant, autumn and winter **Where** Breeds in damp marshes and meadows, bogs, reedbeds. Passage/winter birds on fields, ditches **Confusion species** Jack Snipe, Woodcock **Call** In flight, harsh scratching *skaaatch*

A medium-sized, shy wader with a long straight bill, fairly stripy plumage and dumpy body.

◀ Very quick in flight, lifting off from ground in a zigzag. Dark upperwings and long bill obvious.

'Drumming' (displaying) males sound amazing - the spread tail feathers catch the air to form a deep humming.

◀ The long bill and striped head are often the first things that you'll notice. The delicate markings on the upperparts are exquisite, contrasting with the white and dark barred underparts.

▶ Feeding Snipe are generally seen in quiet muddy corners, early mornings and evenings are best.

Jack Snipe • *Lymnocryptes minimus*

18-20cm, 7in

When Autumn passage migrant and winter visitor. Some also on spring passage **Where** Damp ditches, muddy pools, rough wet meadows **Confusion species** Common Snipe **Call** Seldom heard. Quiet but strong-sounding *gatch* when flushed

◀ Flushed only if you nearly tread on them! They fly off in a straight line (unlike Common Snipe) and go much shorter distances before dropping down again. Notice the short bill and very dark upperparts.

▲ Face pattern looks more open than Common Snipe. Short legs are often bent as they rock up and down and from side to side in distinctive bobbing action.

◀ When seen feeding at distance appear almost black on the upperparts except for rich, gold mantle braces.

◀ A smallish, squat-looking, skulking wader, with a noticeably shorter bill than Snipe. Darker plumage too.

Red-necked Phalarope • *Phalaropus lobatus* 17-19cm, 7in

When Spring birds arrive from May onwards. Elsewhere in spring and particularly autumn **Where** Rare, breeds on tundra-like pools in Northern and Western Isles. Migrants seen on freshwater lakes, pools on coast or inland **Confusion species** Grey Phalarope (autumn only) **Call** A squeaking *cheet*

Slighter, more dainty than Grey Phalarope. Slimmer bills and bodies. Often seen pirouetting on the water.

▶ **Non breeding adults** (back) look ghostly- pale, except for the black eye patch and needle-thin, black bill.

▶ **Females** in **breeding plumage** (left) are brighter than males in spring, with an intense red colour on the neck and brighter golden mantle stripes. **Males** look a little dingier, often with a broken breast band.

▲ **Juveniles** (front) are darker on the head than winter adults and look rather gold and black on the back. Underparts are rather sullied.

Grey Phalarope • *Phalaropus fulicarius* 20-22cm, 9in

When Occasionally in winter storms, but autumn is the best time **Where** Either offshore while sea-watching or on coastal pools or marshes. Sometimes inland lakes **Confusion species** Red-necked Phalarope (autumn only) **Call** Rarely heard. Metallic *zip* given in flight

◀ **Breeding** birds are incredibly rare in Britain (less than ten modern-day records).

▶ **Juveniles** (centre) mimic Red-necked in plumage, much browner and buffier than adults, but lacks obvious mantle and wing stripes.

▶ **Non breeding adult/first-winter** bird most likely to be seen. Like the Red-necked Phalarope, they look very pale, except for the cap and eye patch.Thick bill and structure are a give away.

Pomarine Skua • *Stercorarius pomarinus*

42-50cm, 20in

When Mainly in mid- to late autumn, sometimes in big numbers. Rarer in spring. Some in winter **Where** Almost always coastal, sometimes inland. Frequent large spring passage off Western Isles **Confusion species** Arctic and Great Skua **Call** Silent on migration

▶ **Dark phase** (right) are much scarcer than pale birds. Like dark phase Arctic Skuas these birds are entirely dark below, except for the white underwing patch. Tail projections are not always present on autumn birds.

▶ **Pale phase** (bottom) adult looks heavier than a pale Arctic Skua. The head looks darker, and the yellow nape richer. The breast smudges are more pronounced.

◀ **Juveniles** (centre) appear cold grey-brown all over, with barred underparts and underwing. Note 'double' white underwing flash. Paler and darker juveniles exist, but always show that crucial underwing flash.

Arctic Skua • *Stercorarius parasiticus*

37-44cm, 18in

When Breeding birds appear in early to mid spring. Passage birds frequent in autumn, some in spring **Where** Breeds on boggy moorland in Northern Isles. Otherwise coastal, very rare inland **Confusion species** Pomarine and Long-tailed Skua **Call** Heard only on the breeding grounds, a gull-like *ee-glow*

◀ **Dark phase** (top left and top right flying) shows brown underparts, except for white underwing patches. Smallish head, wedge-shaped tail and central tail projections.

◀ ▶ **Juveniles** (all above and middle right) gingery-looking barred underwings, white underwing patch and white shafts on primaries. Paler juveniles occur, with creamy underparts and paler rumps, while dark juveniles are chocolate-brown all over, except for the wing flash.

◀ **Pale phase** (bottom) yellow flush on nape and off-white underparts to grey-brown rear belly and tail. Same upper- and underwing pattern as **juvenile** (middle).

Long-tailed Skua • *Stercorarius longicaudus*

35-41 cm, 16in

When Birds in spring (sometimes in large numbers), also in autumn **Where** Spring birds off Western Isles (mainly).Autumn birds around coasts, especially east and south-west **Confusion species** Arctic Skua (especially autumn) **Call** Silent on passage

Fairly small, slim seabirds with long slender wings and almost tern-like flight. Twists and dips like a hunting Barn Owl over sea.

▶ **Juveniles** are very variable, coming in pale, intermediate and dark types, but always with cold-looking, heavily-barred underparts and upper tail

▲ **Breeding** adults unmistakable. They have dark caps, ashy-grey upper- parts, dusky bellies, a yellow wash to the breast and amazing long central tail feathers.

Great Skua • *Stercorarius skua*

50-58cm, 23in

When Breeding birds appear at nest sites from early spring onwards. Autumn passage, and some in winter and spring **Where** Breeds on boggy moorland of Northern Isles. Otherwise off coasts, very rare inland **Confusion species** Pomarine Skua, immature large gulls **Call** Heard only on breeding sites - a harsh *gonk*

◀ In flight, the first thing you notice are white wing patches. Heavy build is obvious. Powerful in stormy weather and rarely troubled by rough conditions.

▶ Large, heavy bird, broad wings, shortish tail and powerful bill. Aggressive birds on breeding grounds, dive bombing intruders.

▶ On the ground, brutish look is reinforced. Very powerful-looking bill. Plumage almost entirely chocolate-brown, with darker streaks. Some adults can be paler, with a pale-naped look. Youngsters can look very dark above and warm-brown below. Many birdwatchers know them as Bonxies - their Shetland name.

Black Guillemot • *Cepphus grylle*

32-38cm, 14in

When Breeding birds tend to remain near breeding areas. Others mainly in winter or autumn storms **Where** Nests in coastal crevices. Others seen offshore, or in bays and harbours in north Wales and northern Scotland **Confusion species** None **Call** Breeding males have a *zipp, zipp, zipp* call, fine and pipit-like

◀ In flight, note the bold, round white wing patches on non breeding and breeding birds. Wings are quite stubby and rounded. Will whizz by on a seawatch!

▲ **Non breeding** bird retains white wing patches, otherwise appears white and mealy-grey all over, except for black wings and tail.

▼ **Breeding** birds look stunning. Black all over, except for the bold white wing patches. Bill similar to Guillemot but slimmer and shorter. Legs and feet bright red.

Razorbill • *Alca torda*

38-43cm, 16.5in

When Arrives back in late winter, leaving ledges in late summer/early autumn **Where** Breeds on steep cliffs, often in crevices, in many localities around Britain. Also at sea **Confusion species** Guillemot **Call** Fairly quiet birds, a deep *urrrr* heard on ledges

▼ **Breeding** bird, note black-looking upperparts and intricately marked, deep- based, stout bill. A fine white blaze comes onto head from bill. Underparts show no grey on the flanks.

Slightly stockier and more robust than Guillemot, smaller when seen side by side.

▼ On the water **non breeding** birds look more bull-headed than Guillemot, but shares a whitish- looking face. Tail appears longer and is invariably cocked. Bill pattern becomes duller.

Guillemot • *Uria aalge*

38-46cm, 17.5in

When Arrives back in late winter, leaving ledges in late summer/early autumn **Where** Breeds on steep cliffs around Britain. Also at sea **Confusion species** Razorbill **Call** Low rumbling *mmmm* or a harsh, stacatto *har-har-har-har*

▼ **Breeding** birds have chocolate-brown above, with a fairly slender-looking bill. Some birds have white eye rings (left) and are known as **Bridled Guillemots.** Both have grey marks on flanks.

▶ Flying auks are tricky to separate. Guillemots look pointed at both ends (cigar-shaped) and have a darker underwing than Razorbill. Note the dusky lines on the underwing and dark'armpit'.

▼ **Non breeding** birds have whitish-looking faces, with a narrow neck collar. Much of the autumn and winter are spent at sea.

Little Auk • *Alle alle*

19-21 cm, 8in

When Mid- to late autumn, occasionally in winter **Where** Offshore, and occasionally 'wrecked' birds inland on pools or lakes **Confusion species** Puffin **Call** Silent on passage

Occasionally occur in large numbers. They fly very quickly, low over the water on a whirr of stubby wings. Very black and white, even at distance. Often movements of Little Auks can number many hundreds, even thousands, of birds in just a day or two. The weather is often incredibly rough, with raging gales from the north along with massive seas and wintry showers. They seem undeterred though, as they tenaciously battle their way past, often very close to the shore.

▲ A tiny black and white auk, with a small stubby bill and tiny wings. Most are seen off the east coast. Dark underwings contrast with the white underparts.

▶ Sometimes exhausted birds will sit on the sea or crash inland. Tiny, stubby bill is obvious. Note the fine white streaks on the upperwing and cocked tail.

Puffin • *Fratercula arctica*

28-34cm, 12in

When Arrives back to breed in early spring, leaving in early autumn. Rarely in winter **Where** Nests in burrows on cliffs in northern Britain. Passage birds offshore **Confusion species** Little Auk, larger auks **Call** Deep, curious sounding orrr-ruu. Will raise a smile every time!

◀ In flight, tricky to identify, especially in winter. Resembles small Razorbills - both look stocky, but Puffins are more compact with a dark underwing. Note dark breast band.

▲ **Adult** Puffins (above right) are unmistakable when seen at a breeding colony. Huge, multicoloured bill contrasts with the white face and black upperparts. Note the dark area around the thigh.

▼ **Juveniles** much duller, with a smaller bill and a greyish wash to the face patch.

▶ Instantly recognizable when seen well, with colourful bill and inquisitive nature.

Black Tern • *Chlidonias niger*

22-26cm, 9-10in

When Appears in April and May, with autumn birds from August to October **Where** Coastal lagoons, inland reservoirs and gravel pits **Confusion species** White-winged Black Tern **Call** Soft *keeslk-keeslk* or *klit*

A smallish tern, with a different feeding flight to other terns. Easterly winds in spring can bring in many birds.

▲ **Juvenile** (left), **summer adult** (centre) and **winter adult** (right). Note all show a grey rump.

◀ **Breeding adults** entirely sooty- black from head to belly, with dark grey upperparts. Stout — bill is black, the legs reddish. Undertail is greyish-white.

▶ **Juveniles** have distinctive black cap and bold 'thumbprints' on the breast side. Upperparts are scaled brown.

▶ **Moulting plumage** seen in mid- to late summer. Black around face and breast moults first, but the upperparts remain dark for some while.

White-winged Black Tern • *Chlidonias leucopterus*

22cm, 8in

When Mainly late spring/early summer (adults), also early autumn (juveniles) **Where** Coastal marshes, inland lakes and reservoirs, mainly southern Britain **Confusion species** Black Tern **Call** Low pitched, hard *kee-k* or grating *chree-ee*

Very similar to the commoner Black Tern, but broader-winged in flight, and a shallow tail notch. On the ground, they look shorter-billed and longer-legged.

▶ A flying **adult** (front) shows a lovely contrast between the sooty-black head, body and underwing coverts and the white of the tail rump and upperwing. Outer primaries are greyish, as are the inner secondaries.

▶ **Juveniles** (back) are best identified by their pale wings and rump, contrasting with a dark brown saddle. They also lack the dark breast smudge of Black Tern. The cap is perhaps slightly less obvious on White-winged Black Tern.

◀ The white covert wing patch and whitish primaries are obvious when perched. Note the deep red (almost black) bill and bright red legs.

Common Tern • *Sterna hirundo*

34-37cm, 14in

When Birds arrive from early to mid-April onwards. Passage birds from late summer to late autumn **Where** Breeds in coastal colonies or inland on gravel pits, lakes and reservoirs **Confusion species** Arctic and Roseate Tern **Call** Noisy birds when on breeding sites - calls include loud *kip-kip* and *skii-arr*

◀ In flight **adult** (left) shows dark wedges on the upperwing; **younger** birds (bottom and right) show a dark leading edge to the wing and greyish trailing edge.

▼ **Juvenile** whitish forehead and fairly scalloped upperparts, often a ginger tone apparent. Fairly dark bill, red at the base.

◀ **Breeding** bird has a neat, glossy black cap, long tail streamers, fairly long red legs and a black tip on red bill.

▶ **Non breeding** adult loses its black cap, red bill and tail streamers.They still look fairly stocky though.

Arctic Tern • *Sterna paradisaea*

33-39cm, 15in

When Arrive from late April and leave by the end of September **Where** Breeds at coastal sites in northern Britain. Passage birds inland and coastal **Confusion species** Common Tern **Call** Noisy birds when on breeding sites - calls similar to Common Tern, *kee-or* or *kiik-kiik*

Neat, sleek-looking bird, with shorter bill and legs than Common Tern. Narrower wings. An awesome migrant, flying from Arctic to Antarctic waters for the winter.

◀ In flight, **adult** birds (left) lack the dark primary wedge of Common Tern, **young** (right) have a distinctive white trailing edge to the upperwing.

▲ **Juveniles** more black on the cap than juvenile Commons. Upperparts tend to look greyer and far less gingery. Small bill and short legs are obvious.

▶ **Adults** short, blood-red bill and short red legs. Can look dumpy. Wings paler grey. Comparatively longer tail streamers than Common Tern.

Roseate Tern • *Sterna dougallii*

33-36cm, 15in

When From mid-May onwards. Most leave by end of August. Very rare breeding species **Where** Entirely coastal, on beaches or offshore islands (mainly in Ireland and Northumberland) **Confusion species** Common Tern **Call** A deep, loud *krraachk*

A graceful tern - slim, shortish-winged birds, with long streamers.

▶ Distinctive in flight. **Adults** (left) look very pale above, with long tail streamers. **Juveniles** (right) resemble Common Terns, but have more contrasting upper- parts (like young Sandwich Tern).

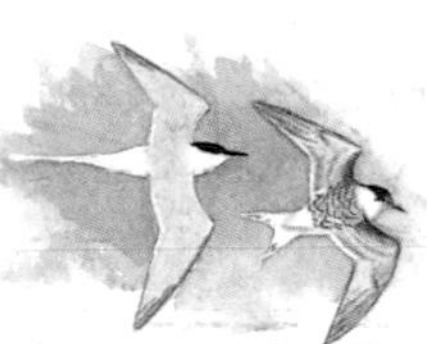

▶ **Juveniles** (back) show an extensive black cap and chequered upper- parts. The bill and legs are black. Reminiscent of juvenile Sandwich Tern.

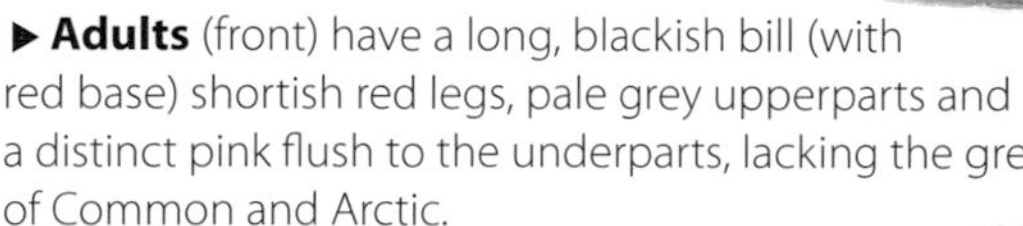

▶ **Adults** (front) have a long, blackish bill (with red base) shortish red legs, pale grey upperparts and a distinct pink flush to the underparts, lacking the grey of Common and Arctic.

Little Tern • *Sterna albifrons*

21-25cm, 9.5in

When Late April onwards, leaving by early autumn **Where** Coastal sites, likes fine shingle. Several breeding sites around the country **Confusion species** None **Call** An excited *kick-ki-kick* or a chattering *kerrie-kit, kerrie-kit, kerrie-kit*

▶ **Non breeding** birds rarely seen here. Bill and legs become dark with less obvious head pattern.

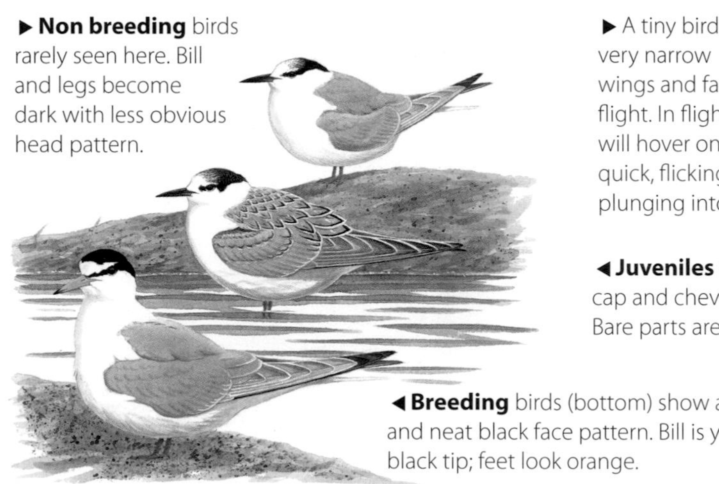

▶ A tiny bird with very narrow wings and fast flight. In flight, will hover on quick, flicking wingbeats, before plunging into the water.

◀ **Juveniles** (centre) have neat black cap and chevron markings on mantle. Bare parts are like a winter adult.

◀ **Breeding** birds (bottom) show a white forehead and neat black face pattern. Bill is yellow with a fine black tip; feet look orange.

Sandwich Tern • *Sterna sandvicensis*

37–43cm, 16.5in

When Arrive from mid-March onwards. Leaves colonies in late summer, rarely winters **Where** Coastal sites, breeds at several large colonies around Britain, unusual inland **Confusion species** Smaller tern species **Call** A grating *keer-rick*. Young begs with a harsh *skreeee-rii*

▶ **Juveniles** (bottom) have finely-marked grey and black upperparts and a black head pattern. Bill lacks pale tip of adults.

▲ In flight, clearly bulkier than other tern species with heavier flight. Even **juveniles** (middle) look white in flight.

◀ **Non breeding** adults lose the shaggy black summer crest, showing a white forehead.

◀ **Breeding** adults (centre) look very pale. Shaggy black head and yellow-tipped black bill.

Kittiwake • *Rissa tridoctyla*

37-42cm, 16in

When Breeding birds return to ledges in early spring. Year round, passage in autumn heavy **Where** Mainly at sea but nests on steep cliffs. Rarely inland, storm driven **Confusion species** Sabine's and Common Gull and juvenile Little Gull **Call** A noisy bird when on cliffs - a nasal onomatopoeic *kitt-i-wake*

The Kittiwake is a neat, small to medium-sized gull, with small head and longish wings.

▶ **Adult** in flight (top) reminiscent of Common Gull, but has paler grey upperparts and small black triangle on the wing tips. They fly with shallower, stiffer beats than many gulls, appearing a little more tern-like than some.

◀ **Juveniles** in flight (above) show a distinctive black M-pattern on the upperwing, with grey and white remainder. Note the black nape and tail bar. This plumage can be confused with the much rarer Sabine's Gull.

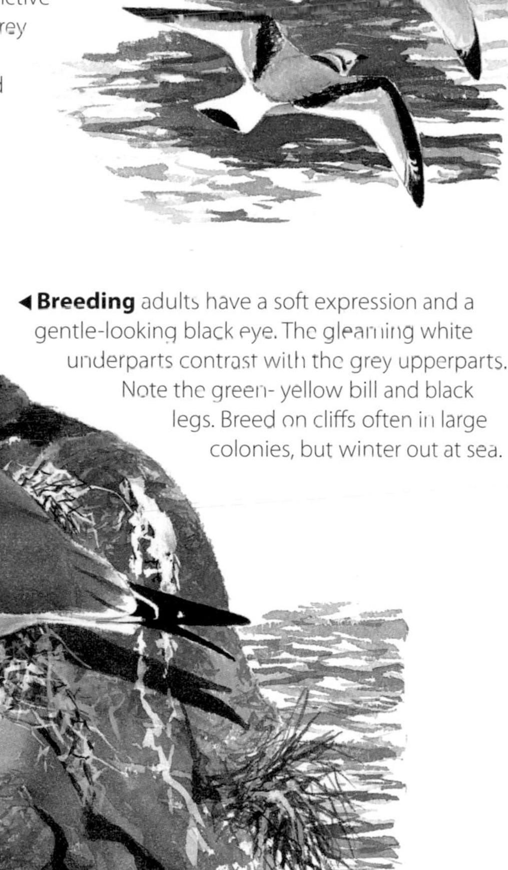

◀ **Breeding** adults have a soft expression and a gentle-looking black eye. The gleaming white underparts contrast with the grey upperparts. Note the green- yellow bill and black legs. Breed on cliffs often in large colonies, but winter out at sea.

Sabine's Gull • *Larus sabini*

30-36cm, 14in

When Mainly in autumn, very rare otherwise **Where** Coastal, in gales, particularly in south-west England and Ireland. Rarer on other coasts **Confusion species** Kittiwake, Little Gull **Call** Not heard

▼**Summer adult** (left), charcoal-grey hood edged black, with yellow tip to dark bill.

A delicate gull, with distinctive plumage. Small-bodied, but large-winged. Notched tail. Striking feature about juveniles and adults is tri-coloured wing patterns.

◀**Juveniles** (top) black on outer wing, with white and scaled grey-brown. Mantle scaled grey-brown, extending to head and breast sides. At distance, head looks hooded, albeit pale in appearance. Notched tail shows black bar.

▲**Adults** share wing pattern of juveniles, with silvery-grey replacing scaled-brown. Mantle also shows grey.

◀ Note difference between ages and similarly-aged **Kittiwakes: juvenile** (right) **adult** (left) - be warned, it looks easy, but in a howling gale with sea spray it is a different story!

Black-headed Gull • *Larus ridibundus*

35-39cm, 14-15in

When Throughout the year **Where** From coastal marshes to inland gravel pits **Confusion species** Little and Mediterranean Gull **Call** Harsh, drawn out *kreeare* or a hard, sharp *kek*

▶ **First-summer** shows a dusky hood.

▶ **Adult summer** shows chocolate-brown hood. Black flight feathers. Pink flush on breast.

▲ In flight, note the upperwing pattern of **a first year** bird (left). On **adults** (right) note the strong white leading edge, with black trailing edge to the outer wing feathers.

◀ **First-winter** mottled head, brown flecking on wings. Bill and legs muddy-orange.

◀ **Adult winter** identical to summer bird except for dark smudges behind the eye and duller bare-parts.

Little Gull • *Larus minutus*

24-28cm, 11 in

When In all months, main numbers in spring and autumn **Where** Coastal lagoons, inland lakes and reservoirs, also at sea **Confusion species** Black-headed and Sabine's Gull, Kittiwake **Call** Contact call between flocks - a sharp *keek*

Very small birds with plump bodies, small heads and rounded wings in flight.

▼ **First summer** bird (top) has a greyish hood with remnants of juvenile plumage on the upper-wings. Short reddish legs.

▲ **Juveniles** in flight (right) appear late summer into mid-autumn. Note dark M on upperwing, the dark cap, mantle and tail bar. Note **adults'** (left) dark underwing.

◀ **Juveniles** show dark cap and dark eye spot. The very short bill and legs are deep red.

◀ **Breeding** adults have neat black hoods, silvery upperwings and dark underwings. Note outermost white primary tips.

Mediterranean Gull • *Larus melanocephalus*

37-40cm, 15in

When Breeders appear in late winter. Throughout the year, flocks in winter **Where** Nests in gull colonies on coasts. Also seen along seafronts, piers, and at inland and coastal roosts **Confusion species** Black-headed Gull, young Common Gull **Call** A far-carrying, repeated, Chough-like *yoow*

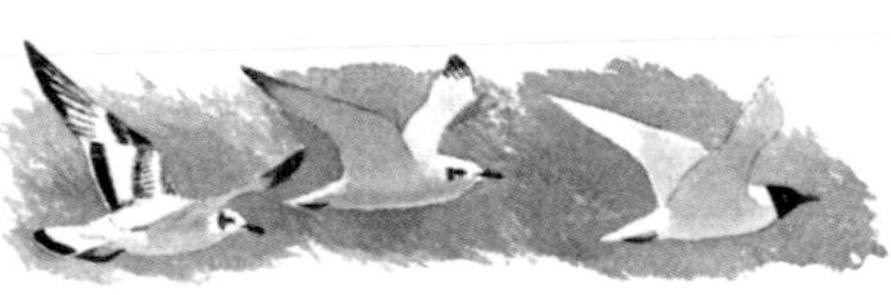

▲ **Breeding** adults (far left) have black hoods, more silvery upperwing and white wingtips. **Second winter** birds (centre) show variable amounts of black on primaries and around eye. **First winters** (right) like Common Gulls, but paler grey on wings and mantle. Note the tail band and eye patch.

▲ **Non breeding winter** adults (rear) lose black hoods, but show a distinctive dark eye patch. Thickish bill is deep-red, some more yellow and black on tip. Longish leg length too. **First winter** (front) has a dark bill and legs and dark mask.

Great Black-backed Gull • *Larus marinus*

61-78cm, 31 in

When Year round **Where** Breeds on coastal cliffs **Confusion species** Lesser Black-backed Gull **Call** Similar to Herring and Lesser Black-backed but deeper pitch

The largest gull, with a bulky appearance and hefty bill. Takes four years to reach maturity.

▶ In flight, **juveniles** (far left) look big. The plumage appears a little paler than other dark-backed large gulls. **Adults** (left) look jet black across the wings.

▼ On the ground, size is very striking. Huge head and yellow bill of the **adult** (top) will be obvious, as will the back colour.

▼ **Juveniles** (middle) look quite grey and white at a distance but up close, note the black feather centres and very white head.

◀ **Second winter** (bottom) shows some adult feathers on mantle. Head and underparts are very white, unlike other larger gulls.

Lesser Black-backed Gull • *Larus fuscus* 48-56cm, 22in

When Throughout the year, particularly in summer and autumn **Where** Coastal areas, also inland, especially pig fields, rubbish tips and fields **Confusion species** Herring, Great Black-backed and Yellow-legged Gull **Call** Like Herring Gull, but deeper

▶ Flying **juvenile** (left) far darker tail than young Herring Gull; also much darker on the upperwing, lacking a 'window'. Plumage is greyer toned. **Adult** (right) shows small white tips to the primaries and ashy grey upperparts.

▶ Structurally, they look slimmer, longer-winged and neater and better proportioned than the bulkier Herring Gull. All ages have a rather soft expression when compared to Herring Gull, a feature that becomes more obvious, the more familiar you become with larger gull identification.

▶ The Lesser Black-backed Gull is a neat-looking four-year-stage large gull, smaller than its confusion species. An **adult** (top) has a slimmer bill than the Herring Gull and is far less hefty overall than the Great Black-backed. Colour of the wings can vary from ashy-grey to almost black (the darker the bird the further north its origins – Norwegian birds are recorded annually in UK) but always darker than Herring Gull. Note the yellow legs.

▶ **Juvenile** (right) appears greyer than young Herring Gull, while young Great Black-backeds look very different. Note the different feather patterns on the wing.

▶ **First-summer/ second-winter** bird (bottom) already has ashy- grey feathers coming through on its mantle, but retains lots of immature streaking.

Herring Gull • *Larus argentatus*

54–67cm, 26in

When Year round **Where** Coastal areas, also inland, especially at rubbish tips **Confusion species** Other large gulls **Call** Loud, far carrying *kee-yow*

Large gull, with four different age-groups as they reach adulthood. In northern and eastern Britain, along with many Irish coasts, the winter population of British Herring Gulls is swollen by the larger Scandinavian Herring Gull *(argentatus).* Adults are darker grey on the back and wings, while the wing tips generally show far more white than British adults do. Younger birds can be picked out by practised eyes, some first winter birds can look really distinctive and pale, almost like dark-winged Glaucous Gulls.

▲In flight, both **juveniles** (left) and **adults** (right) are easily identified. Juveniles look very brown above, notice the dark trailing edge and pale 'window' (between secondaries and primaries) on the upperwing. Adults are white-headed in summer, with pale grey upperparts. Herring Gulls are larger than Lesser Black- backed, but smaller than Great Black-backed.

▼**Adults** (top) show small white tips on the black primaries. The eye is pale yellow, and the legs pink. A bird in its **first-summer** plumage (middle) shows grey on the mantle, mixed with juvenile plumage. The older they become, the more young feathers are replaced.

◀**Juveniles** (bottom) look greyish-brown all over with distinctive patterning on the upperparts and wings.

Yellow-legged Gull • *Larus michahellis*

52-58cm, 22in

When Throughout the year, many in late summer and winter **Where** Coastal marshes, beaches, inland lakes, reservoirs and rubbish tips **Confusion species** Caspian and Herring Gull **Call** Similar to Lesser Black-backed Gull, rather deep and nasal in tone

A relatively 'new' species, structurally similar to Herring Gull (of which it was long considered a sub-species).

▶ **Summer adult,** upperparts dark blue-grey, wingtips black. Head and underparts white. Yellow eye with narrow blood-red orbital ring. Stout, thick-looking legs are custard-yellow. Winter adult similar, except for head streaking.

▲ **Third-winters,** distinctive blue- grey feathers on mantle or upperwing from **second year.** Legs yellow from second year.

▶ **Juveniles** and **first winters** resemble pale Lesser Black-backeds, I whitish heads, heavy black bill, streaked under parts and dark upperwings, hint of a pale window as Herring. Rump is whitish, with a broad black tail band.

Caspian Gull • *Larus cachinnans*

52-58cm, 22in

When Tends to be in winter, with a few summer/early autumn birds **Where** Inland lakes, reservoirs and rubbish tips, coastal marshes **Confusion species** Yellow- legged and Herring Gull **Call** Rather loud, almost laughing squawk - not unlike a donkey braying

▼ **Adult,** sloping head, dark eye and silvery-grey upperparts. Bolder white-tips on primaries than Yellow-legged, note different pattern on underwing – this can be crucial! Long legs are greyish- pink to dull-flesh in colour, lacking the brightness of other similar species.

▲ **Juvenile/first winter,** pronounced 'snouty'- look, narrow, long black bill with whitish-looking head. Upperparts resemble Yellow-legged, but more finely patterned and more sepia-toned. Tail band is broader than Yellow-legged, and underwing paler. Legs are dull pink.

▲ Bill less boldly-coloured than other gulls, pale-yellow with a dull- red spot.

Iceland Gull • *Larus glaucoides* 52-60cm, 23in

When Occurs in late autumn, through the winter **Where** Coastal fish ports, rubbish tips (coastal and inland). Mainly west coast of Britain and Ireland **Confusion species** Glaucous Gull, large albino gulls **Call** Slightly higher-pitched than Herring Gull

◀ ▼ **Juveniles** (right and below) are biscuit-brown, with buff-white wingtips and bi-coloured bills. Become paler as they get older, whitish in second year, and grey-backed by third winter.

▼ **Non breeding** (left) streaked head, but otherwise resembles **breeding** bird (right), complete with soft grey-toned back, yellow bill and white wingtips.

▲ Smaller than Glaucous, with a softer expression, better proportions and longer wings. Four years to reach maturity

Glaucous Gull • *Larus hyperboreus* 63-68cm, 24in

When Occurs from late autumn and throughout the winter **Where** Coastal fish ports, rubbish tips (coastal and inland). Mainly west coast of Britain and Ireland **Confusion species** Iceland Gull, albino large gulls **Call** Similar to Herring Gull, deeper pitch

◀ **Juveniles** are biscuit-brown, with buff-white wingtips and bi-coloured bills, becoming paler as they get older, whitish in their second year, and grey-backed by their third.

▼ **Adult winter** (rear) lots of streaking on head, otherwise resembles **summer adult** (front). Mantle paler grey than Herring Gull; white wingtips. **Juvenile** in flight (right).

▶ A brute of a bird, with four age groups to maturity. Big bills, large heads and chunky bodies. They look fairly short-winged.

Common Gull • *Larus canus*

40-46cm, 17in

When Throughout the year, much commoner in winter **Where** Breeds in northern England, Scotland and Ireland in damp meadows and pools. In winter seen on coastal and inland waters **Confusion species** Mediterranean Gull (first year only) **Call** Always high-pitched *ke ke ke kleyah*

◀ **First winter** heavily-streaked breast and head. Dark grey mantle, brown coverts and tertials on wings.

▶ In flight, **first winter.** Note streaked, brown head, dark grey mantle, distinctive upperwing pattern, barred white rump and broad black tail band.

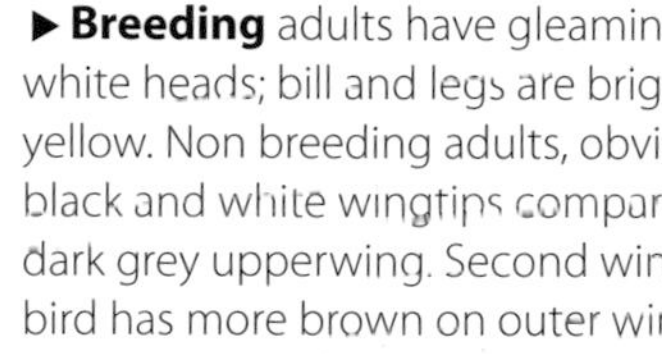

▶ **Breeding** adults have gleaming white heads; bill and legs are bright yellow. Non breeding adults, obvious black and white wingtips compared to dark grey upperwing. Second winter bird has more brown on outer wing and heavy greyish blotching on the head.

Ring-billed Gull • *Larus delawarensis*

41-49cm, 16.5-19in

When Mainly winter, but some present all year **Where** Lakes, rivers, estuaries, beaches, particularly in Ireland and south-west England. **Confusion species** Common Gull **Call** Not unlike a Herring Gull, but higher-pitched and more nasal

◀ **Second winter,** bill has broad, black band and yellow/ green tip. Head streaking distinctive, coarser and less dense than Common.

▶ A flying **first-winter** has paler area of grey on saddle and wing than Common. Brown on forewing less densely marked. Stouter bill more bi-coloured too.

Stockier than Common Gull, with a thicker bill. First recorded in Britain in 1973, now seen in some numbers every year, some birds semi-resident.

◀ **Adult winter** yellow bill, paler tip, with black band. Head streaking less dense than Common. Note the paler iris. Lacks white edges to tertials, less white on wingtips. Yellowish legs.

Rock Dove • *Columba livia*

29-35cm, 13.5in

When Throughout the year **Where** Cliffs and fields of northern Scotland and Ireland **Confusion species** Feral Pigeon (small percentage resemble Rock Dove) **Call** Much as Feral Pigeon, a low pitched *coo-ooo-ooo*

Rock Doves have undergone something of a dramatic decline over recent years. Feral Pigeon populations have soared in regions once the stronghold of wild Rock Doves.

▲ Genuine Rock Doves occur in western Scotland and Ireland only, around coastal fields and cliffs. White rump and black wing bars are obvious. Can be hard to separate from coastal Feral Pigeons, which have originated from wild stock over the years.

▼ More rugged and robust than feral stock. Pale-grey forewings, unlike chequered Ferals. Most striking features are the white rump and the double black wing bars.

Feral Pigeon • *Columba livia*

29-35cm, 14in

When Throughout the year **Where** Across almost any built-up area of the country. Less common in countryside **Confusion species** Rock Dove **Call** A rather monotonous, low *coo-coo-ooo*

▶ A familiar, round-looking dove that has managed to infiltrate the Rock Dove population of Britain, with a drastic effect on the wild, pure stock.

Coming in an incredible variety of different plumages, colours varying from white to black, and brown to grey, with a mix of different combinations and patterns.

▲ This bird is fairly close to the true Rock Dove. Blue-grey head merges into a metallic- green sheen on the neck. Upper breast shows a purple gloss.

Stock Dove • *Columba oenas*

28-32cm, 11-12.5in

When Throughout the year **Where** Woods and open farmland across Britain and Ireland, absent in northern areas **Confusion species** Woodpigeon **Call** A low-pitched, monotonous *coo-oh, coo-oh*

Smaller than Woodpigeon, with a small, squarish head, plump body and beautifully subtle plumage. It never shows the more obvious white neck patch of adult Woodpigeons and, unlike the latter, has two short dark bars across the inner wing.

◀ Grey upperparts, except for black on the coverts and primaries. Tail shows a broad black tip. Dark silvery- grey head with an emerald-green neck patch and salmon-pink breast. Underparts can be quite variable in colour, but are generally grey, sometimes looking quite blue. Bill is pale yellow, with a whitish 'knob' and reddish base.

Woodpigeon • *Columba palumbus*

38-43cm, 15-17in

When Year round **Where** Woodland, parkland, farmland across the country **Confusion species** Stock Dove **Call** Throaty-sounding *hoo-hrooah*

▶ **Juveniles** lack the white neck patch. Breast is duller, showing a more buff-pink colour.

▶ In flight, note the white neck-collar, large white wing patches and dark tail.

A familiar, plump bird with a small head, full-chest, broad wings and a longish tail. In autumn, hundreds of birds can be seen in agricultural areas - the numbers swollen by continental immigrants too.

▶ **Adults** are pale blue-grey above, with a greenish gloss on the hindneck, a white neck patch and blue-grey nape and rump. The breast is purplish-pink, fading to pale grey-white on the belly.

Collared Dove • *Streptopelia decaocto* 31-34cm, 13in

When Throughout the year **Where** Almost any habitat around the country, from secluded countryside to noisy cities **Confusion species** Turtle Dove **Call** A soft *coo-coo-kut*

◀ In flight, note the black wing tips and the tail pattern, white tips to all but the central feathers, with black-grey at the base.

▼ Broad-winged and long-tailed with sandy- brown plumage. Introduced into Europe from Asia in mid 1900s. By the early 1950s, the first birds were seen in Britain and are now widespread.

▶ **Adults** (left) are brownish on the upperparts and buff-pink below. Distinctive black and white collar on the neck. The closed tail looks greyish, with buff and white outer feathers. Some birds can appear very pale. **Juveniles** (right) lack the neck collar and are scalier on the upperparts.

Turtle Dove • *Streptopelia turtur* 25-27cm, 10in

When Arrives from late April, leaving by early October **Where** Increasingly scarce, woodland, plantations and bushy hedgerows **Confusion species** Collared Dove **Call** A soft, deep purring *rrroooooorrr, rrroooooorrr*

▶ **Juveniles** show a buff head, no neck bars and more subdued, duller brown wing markings.

▶ **Adults'** heads are grey with a buff-pink face. Neck shows several black bars with distinctive white edges. Wings are rich-chestnut with bold black feather centres.

▲ Pinkish grey breast, fading to off-white or pale- grey on the flanks and belly. Upperwing grey, chestnut, black and white clashing in a flurry of colour. Note grey rump with the black and white tail.

Common Cuckoo • *Cuculus canorus*

32-36cm, 13in

When Arrives in April, leaving by September **Where** Countrywide, from woods to reedbeds, coastal dunes to moorland **Confusion species** Kestrel, Hobby, Merlin **Call** Far-carrying, familiar *cuc-coo* also a stuttering *cuc-cuc-oo* and when agitated, a gargling, laughing *gug-gug-gug-gug*

▲ **Juveniles,** once fledged, still take advantage of the surrogate parents' hospitality. Their plumage appears very scaly above and barred below.

▲ **Females'** hepatic (brown or red) phase is far scarcer than typical grey females. Most of the upperparts, except for the primaries, are rufous with fine black barring from head to tail. Females' grey phase is identical to males', except for a brown wash on the breast and browner- looking flight feathers.

▶ In flight, wings are never lifted above body level. Pointed wings and long tail obvious in flight.

◀ Medium-sized, slim-looking birds, with pointed wings and a long tail. Entirely grey upperparts, darker on the wings. Tail is dark grey, with white notches on each tail feather. Underparts are barred black and white.

Ring-necked Parakeet • *Psittacula krameri*

39-43cm, 17in

When Throughout the year, best looked for in winter **Where** Breeds in wooded areas and parks in several south-eastern counties. Birds elsewhere probably escapees **Confusion species** European Bee-eater, other escaped parakeets (e.g. Alexandrine's) **Call** Raucous, loud squawking *keeyik, keeyik, keeyik*

▲ The Ring-necked Parakeet has established itself as a thriving colonist, after a number escaped during the 1950s and '60s. Medium-sized birds with slim wings and long tail.

▶ Pretty, unmistakable birds, but note the collar is present only on males. The bill is red, the tail and underwing are green. Winter flocks with many hundreds of birds can be seen in London suburbs.

Barn Owl • *Tyto alba*

33-39cm, 13-15in

When Year round **Where** Open countryside, scrubby areas, ditches and woodland fringes **Confusion species** None **Call** A variety of eerie shrieks, squeals and purrs - uttered by both sexes, either flying or perched. Young birds beg with a wheezy snore

A medium-sized owl with slim body and longish wings. Gradually re-establishing themselves after a serious decline in the 1980s.

◀ A ghostly apparition drifting over the fields showing broad, rounded wings, yellow-buff upperparts, barred tail and white underwings.

▲ **Adults** work hard to keep their offspring nourished, flying at any time of day in the breeding season to hunt.

◀ **Adults** have heart-shaped face with a thin grey border. Upperparts are rich yellow-orange, mixed with greys, blacks and browns. The short tail shows three grey bars.

Little Owl • *Athene noctua*

23-27.5cm, 9-10.5in

When Throughout the year **Where** Open farmland and parkland in England and Wales **Confusion species** None **Call** Feline-like *kee-uw* or, during the breeding season, a variety of canine-like yelps and even barks

▶ A distinctive head pattern with boldly marked chocolate upper- and underparts. The short square tail is barred brown and white. When seen head on, the striking, fierce bright yellow eyes are particularly obvious. The white stripes around the head give the bird an almost grumpy look.

A small, squat, broad-headed bird with a short tail. Introduced in Britain towards the end of the 19th century. More active in daylight than other owls.

▲ In flight, the rounded wings and undulating flight (reminiscent of woodpeckers or Mistle Thrush) are obvious.

Tawny Owl • *Strix aluco*

37-43cm, 16in

When Throughout the year **Where** Open countryside, woodland, parkland and gardens across the country. Absent in Ireland **Confusion species** None **Call** *Too-wit, too woo* call is *the* owl call, but is actually closer to being a long, drawn-out *oo-ooo-hooo*.Also a loud, penetrating *kee-wick*

▼ Mainly nocturnal, medium-sized, plump owl with a longish body. Plumage varies from reddish-brown to grey-brown. Upperparts are warm-brown, with many black vermiculations. Underparts have a brown wash to the breast and flanks.

▶ In flight, round-winged and square-tailed. Underwing appears barred with black and white on the flight feathers.

◀ **Juveniles** have large black eyes peering out from a mass of down and feathers.

Short-eared Owl • *Asio flammeus*

33–40cm, 15.5in

When Breeds in northern Britain, rarely in south. Passage birds arrive in mid-autumn onwards **Where** Breeds on moorland and young conifer plantations. Passage/ wintering birds around coasts and reedbeds **Confusion species** Long-eared Owl **Call** Usually silent

A long-winged, medium-sized owl often seen during daylight hours, particularly in winter. Far more likely to be seen hunting than the closely related Long-eared Owl.

◀ In flight, there are clear differences from Long-eared Owl. Short-eared Owls have more black on primaries and the upperwing shows clear white trailing edge. Primary patches on the upperwing tend to appear yellow, rather than orange of Long-eared. Underparts are streaked only to the breast.

▼ On the ground, the small ear tufts are barely visible. The face appears less richly coloured than Long-eared and the eyes are fiercely yellow. The teardrop marks on the breast are easily seen.

Long-eared Owl • *Asio otus*

31–37cm, 12–14.5in

When Passage birds appear in mid-to late autumn. Winters in roosts **Where** Breeds in woodlands and conifer plantations near open areas of farmland. Wintering birds inland and coastal. Common in Ireland
Confusion species Short-eared Owl
Call A deep repeated *oh* from adults, Youngsters have a high-pitched, squeaky *pee-eeh*

A secretive bird, mainly nocturnal. Smaller than Tawny, just smaller than Short-eared.

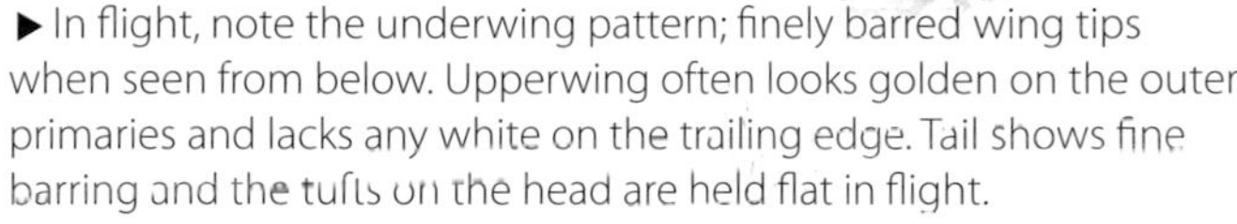

▶ In flight, note the underwing pattern; finely barred wing tips when seen from below. Upperwing often looks golden on the outer primaries and lacks any white on the trailing edge. Tail shows fine barring and the tufts on the head are held flat in flight.

▶ When perched and alert, the long ear tufts will be raised. The face, upper- and underparts are warmer-toned than Short-eared Owl and underparts more boldly marked. Note the bright orange eyes.

Nightjar • *Caprimulgus europaeus*

24-28cm, 10in

When Arrive on breeding grounds in mid-May, leaving in early autumn **Where** Breeds on heathland and low plantations. Passage birds on coasts **Confusion species** None **Call** A hard churring, sometimes relentless through the night. Also a sharp, but mellow, *too-wick*

Fairly unmistakable in flight and seen mainly before dusk. Rarely seen in daylight hours.

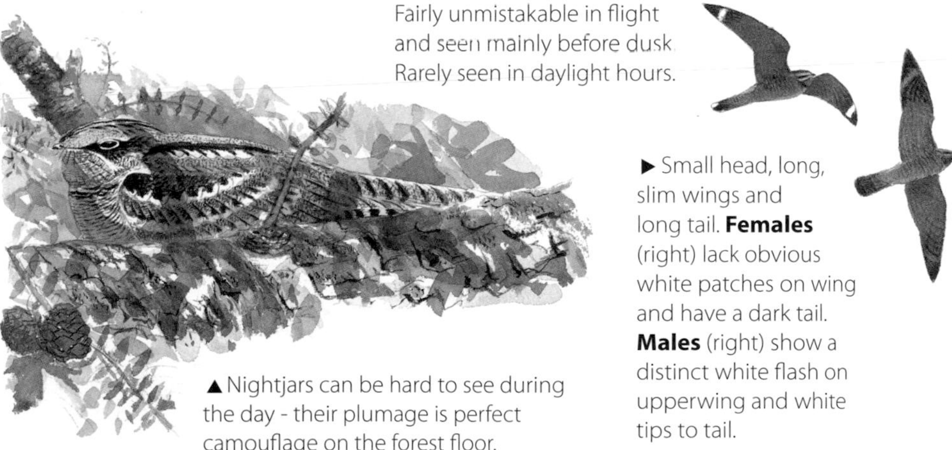

▲ Nightjars can be hard to see during the day - their plumage is perfect camouflage on the forest floor.

▶ Small head, long, slim wings and long tail. **Females** (right) lack obvious white patches on wing and have a dark tail. **Males** (right) show a distinct white flash on upperwing and white tips to tail.

Common Swift • *Apus apus*

17-18.5cm, 7.5in

When Arrives from mid-April onwards, leaves during late August to September **Where** Almost anywhere, from quiet country villages to the noisiest city **Confusion species** None **Call** A piercing, shrill scream, often heard from flocks in late summer

◀ With scythe-shaped wings, short- looking forked tail and generally dark brown plumage, the Swift is fairly unmistakable. Competent fliers, Swifts display a wide variety of shapes when airborne.

▲ A familiar summertime sight, parties of screaming Swifts careering over rooftops, sometimes even below head height, but always in control.

◀ **Juveniles** appear browner and more scaly than adults, with a more extensive white throat bib.

▲ Perched on a wall, they look ungainly.

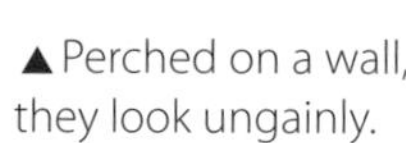

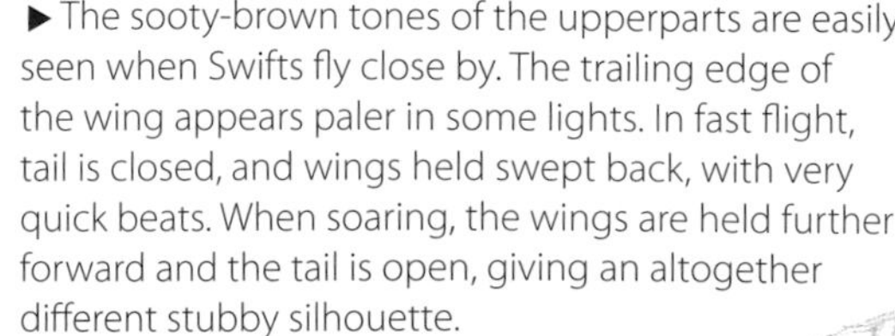

▶ The sooty-brown tones of the upperparts are easily seen when Swifts fly close by. The trailing edge of the wing appears paler in some lights. In fast flight, tail is closed, and wings held swept back, with very quick beats. When soaring, the wings are held further forward and the tail is open, giving an altogether different stubby silhouette.

Common Kingfisher • *Alcedo atthis*

17-19.5cm, 7in

When Throughout the year **Where** Rivers, streams, lakes and gravel pits, countrywide except Scotland **Confusion species** None **Call** Ringing *peeep, peeep*

An instantly recognizable bird with a large head, thick-based dagger-like bill, short wings and a short tail.

▶ Will fly past in a whoosh of psychedelic colour. Blue upperparts contrast with greener flight feathers and the orange underparts.

◀ The classic view of a Kingfisher - plunging into the water with wings held back, neck extended, bill thrusting forward and then, SPLASH!

◀ **Males** have all black bill, while females have a reddish base to bill. Juveniles' (bottom) colours are more subdued.

▶ Kingfishers have a habit of sitting motionless on a branch for some while. When perched they will bob their heads and flick their tails before whirring off at great speed.

Hoopoe • *Upupa epops*

25-29cm, 12in

When Appears from mid-April into June. Also in mid-autumn **Where** A very rare breeding migrant, Hoopoes breed in copses around open land. Passage birds can appear anywhere, mainly southern Britain **Confusion species** Jay **Call** Most likely to hear song, repeated *poo-poo-poo-poo*

◀ In flight, Hoopoes resemble giant floppy butterflies, with distinctive undulating, dipping flight.

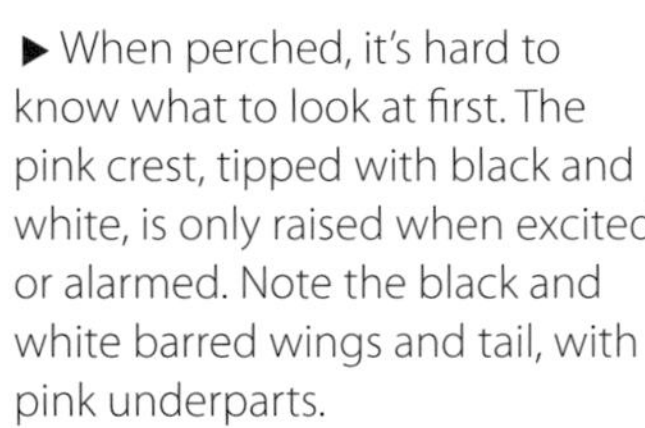

▶ When perched, it's hard to know what to look at first. The pink crest, tipped with black and white, is only raised when excited or alarmed. Note the black and white barred wings and tail, with pink underparts.

◀ A very pretty and generally unmistakable bird if seen well, Hoopoes have very striking plumage, a distinctive down-turned bill and floppy flight. The salmon pink body contrasts strongly with the bold black and white patterning of the wings and tail. Hoopoes feed on the ground with a somewhat low-slung, shuffling gait and they are very found of a good lawn!

European Bee-eater • *Merops apiaster*

29cm, 12in

When Mainly spring and early summer, occasional autumn records **Where** Very rare breeding migrant, favours open country with perches. Often in southern Britain **Confusion species** Ring-necked Parakeet **Call** A rather soft, repeated, rolling *purrt*

A Mediterranean migrant, uncommon but almost annual visitor, occasionally in flocks. Medium-sized bird, with amazing plumage and very distinctive habits.

▲ Upperside reveals blue- grey primaries and rump. Underwing pale, with dark trailing edge and pale-blue body. Often glides slowly in circles, before plunging and dipping quickly for passing food.

▶ Conspicuous plumage of rich-chestnut head and mantle, broad black eyestripe, yellow throat patch and sky-blue under parts. A good view will reveal yellow on lower back, chestnut on wings and long, narrow tail feathers. Stout, decurved bill.

Wryneck • *Jynx torquilla*

16-18cm, 7in

When Can appear from early April into early summer. Mainly in autumn **Where** Passage birds tend to appear on coasts, particularly in east and south of UK **Confusion species** None **Call** Rarely heard, the song is a falcon-like *kee-kee-kee*

▼ A small (warbler-sized) member of the wood pecker family, although you are more likely to encounter one on the ground. Pretty unmistakable, with amazing plumage and sharp bill.

▲ Wrynecks are a mass of subtle, earthy tones and the most intricate of vermiculations. Most striking are the yellowish throat, the dark band on the mantle and brownish wings.

Green Woodpecker • *Picus viridis*

30-36cm, 12-14in

When Throughout the year **Where** Woodland, gardens, fields around Britain. Absent in northern Scotland and whole of Ireland **Confusion species** Golden Oriole (female only) **Call** A laughing yaffle *yaah-yaah-yaaah*

A long, robust-looking bird, with a powerful, sharp bill, large grey feet (two toes forward, two toes back) and a short, spiky tail, which the bird uses as a psuedo-crampon on a tree trunk.

▲ In flight, they have an undulating manner. Deep beats are followed by closed wings as the bird progresses. As they approach a tree, they arrive with a huge upward sweep before landing on a trunk.

▲ **Juveniles** are heavily streaked and barred on the underparts and have less vivid red heads.

▶ **Males** have red centres to the moustache. Both sexes have a dull- yellow rump and uppertail-coverts, while the graduated tail is brown- grey with darker bars.

◀ **Females** have wholly black moustache. Cheeks and throat are pale greyish-white to pale yellow.

Great Spotted Woodpecker • *Dendrocopos major* 24cm, 10in

When Throughout the year **Where** Woods, parks and copses around Britain. Absent from Ireland **Confusion species** Lesser Spotted Woodpecker **Call** An explosive, excited *chick*. In spring, males have a very loud, rapid drum, faster than any other woodpecker

◀ A medium-sized woodpecker with pied plumage, thick pointed bill, graduated tail and 'reverse' toes.

▲ **Males** (above) have a red nape, absent on **female** (right). Both sexes share bold black and white patterning on upperparts, along with bold red patches on the undertail. Note the longer central tail feathers, essential for balance when the bird is on a tree.

▲ In flight, particularly striking. The bold white shoulder patches and white spotting on the wings really stand out. Like other woodpeckers 'Great Spots' have undulating flight.

▶ **Juvenile** 'Great Spots' similar to adults, with red crowns and rather more sullied underparts.

Lesser Spotted Woodpecker • *Dendrocopos minor* 15cm, 6in

When Year round, best in late winter and early spring **Where** Woods and parks, mainly in southern England. Absent from Scotland and Ireland **Confusion species** Great Spotted Woodpecker **Call** An excited Kestrel-like *kee-kee-kee*. Drumming fairly weak

Same size as a House Sparrow (Europe's smallest woodpecker), with neat pied plumage, small sharp bill, and the familiar graduated tail and reverse toes of the group.

▲ In flight, typically undulating, with striking barring on the back and wings.

▶ **Females** in breeding plumage, have a whitish crown and lack any red markings.

◀ **Males** have neat red crown, compared with the whitish crown of the female. Upperparts are barred black and white, with off-white underparts. There is no red on the underparts, unlike Great Spotted Woodpecker.

▼ **Juveniles** resemble adults, with a whitish forehead, flecked black, spottier flanks and a buff wash to the face.

Sky Lark • *Alauda arvensis*

16-18cm, 7in

When Throughout the year. Passage migrant **Where** Found from moorland to coastal grazing meadows. Open land and stubble fields in autumn **Confusion species** Wood Lark, Shore Lark, Lapland Bunting **Call** A rolling *prruup.* Sings from great height at most times of the year, a marvellous mix of fluty, mellifluous notes

◀ In flight, Sky Larks look pale brown, with an obvious white trailing edge to the wing and white outer feathers on the longish tail. Upperwing is more contrasting than Wood Lark and Shore Lark.

▼ Fairly large, rotund lark, which feeds low to the ground, shuffling along in autumn and winter flocks (sometimes in many hundreds).

▼ Worn birds in winter and early spring flatten their crests, and look rather indistinct. Much individual variation, from greyish to warm, brown-looking birds like this.

▶ When disturbed or alarmed Sky Larks will raise their crests. The distinctive breast pattern can be compared with the confusion species, and note the chunky, stubby bill and longish tail.

Wood Lark • *Lullula arborea*

13.5-15 cm, 6 in

When Year round. Often wintering near breeding areas, before returning in March **Where** Open heathland and forests, clearings in mixed or broad-leaved woodland, mainly in southern England. Passage birds anywhere, mainly autumn **Confusion species** Sky Lark **Call** Singing birds (flying in bat-like display) have a sweet, descending *lee-lee-leelee-leelee-leeoooleeoo*. Flight call *loo-eet*

▼ Head pattern is very obvious. White supercilia are broad and meet on rear crown.The warm brown ear covert-patch is bold, as is the black and white wing patch. Small bill and shortish tail.

A smallish, rotund, short-tailed lark, formerly a rare breeding species, now increasing annually in numbers.

▲ In flight, note the short tail and dumpy body.Tail has white only on tips, wing lacks a white trailing edge. A black and white patch is a characteristic feature on the forewing.

Shore Lark • *Eremophilia alpestris*

16-19cm, 7.5in

When Arrives from October onwards, leaves in March-April **Where** Almost always on shingle coastlines and saltmarsh. Occasionally stubble fields **Confusion species** Sky Lark **Call** A thin, ringing *tseeh* or *eeeh-deedoo*

Neat and compact, smaller than Sky Lark, with more colourful plumage. Quite common in winter, numbers have fluctuated drastically in past twenty years.

▲ Familiar view over saltmarsh. Broad-winged, with squared tail, you may see face markings on brighter birds. Sandy-brown in flight, with dark tail sides and white outer tail feathers. Lacks white trailing edge.

◀ **Females** (right) duller than **males** (left). Patterning the same for both, males always appear brighter yellow on face, with black horns; becoming more pronounced as spring approaches.

Sand Martin • *Riparia riparia*

12-13cm, 5in

When Arrives from March onwards, leaving by October **Where** Breeds in sandy banks, often fairly close to water. Widespread around coasts in spring and autumn **Confusion species** House Martin, Swallow **Call** Often very vocal in feeding parties and at nest sites. A dry, almost rolling trrss, which, when the birds get excited, is combined in a series of repeated phrases

A small member of the Swallow family. The breeding population crashed dramatically in the 1980s, but numbers are now building up slowly.

▲ Distinctive in flight - they look rather weak on the wing and, from below, a brown breast band is obvious, as is the shallow notch in the short tail. From above, note the brown upperparts and lack of white on the rump.

▶ Gregarious birds, breeding in colonies and feeding in large groups over water (be it inland reservoirs or coastal reedbeds). In the late summer and early autumn, they roost in large groups in reedbeds, both inland and at the coast.

Swallow • *Hirundo rustica*

17-21 cm, 8in

When Arrives from mid-April onwards, leaving by early October **Where** From coastal marshes to urban streets. Reedbeds in autumn **Confusion species** Sand and House Martin **Call** A tinkling *vit vit* or occasional *splee-plink*. Male's song, a strong, rather fast, twittering warble

◀ Graceful fliers, note the white forewing, pale belly and the white spots on the underside of the deeply-forked tail.

▲ In the autumn, look out for Swallows congregating on telegraph wires.

▲ **Juveniles are** duller than adults, above and be low. The tail streamers are very short.Very young fledglings show flecks of down on the head and a strong yellow gape.

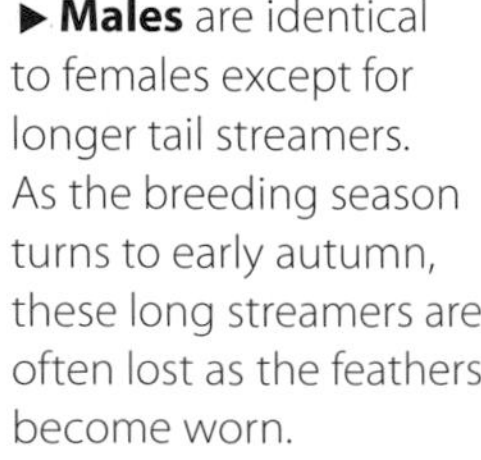

▶ **Males** are identical to females except for longer tail streamers. As the breeding season turns to early autumn, these long streamers are often lost as the feathers become worn.

House Martin • *Delichon urbica* 13.5-15cm, 6in

When Arrives from late April onwards, leaving by October **Where** Nests under the eaves of houses in both rural and urban areas **Confusion species** Sand Martin, Swallow **Call** A dry, rolling *preeet*

▼**Juveniles** (left) are dull versions of **adults** (right), appearing browner on the head and wings, and duller blue on the upperparts. Underparts are off-white. Dingy wash to the throat. Very young fledglings show a yellowish gape at the base of the bill.

▲Favourite nesting sites for House Martins are under the eaves of houses, returning year after year to the same building.

◀Clearly smaller and more compact than the Swallow, House Martins have broad wings, a shortish, notched tail and almost pied-looking plumage.

▶In flight, note the blue-toned broad wings and notched tail contrasting with a square white rump.

Yellow Wagtail • *Motacilla flava* 15-16cm, 6in

When First birds appear from April onwards. Spring and autumn passage sometimes heavy **Where** Breeds in damp meadows and pasture, both inland and coastal. Scarce in Scotland and Ireland **Confusion species** Grey Wagtail, rare pipits (autumn only) **Call** Hard sounding *tsweep*

▲In flight, greenish above, with dark wings and long tail.

▶ **Black-headed Wagtail** *(feldegg)* very rare, usually seen in the Balkans and Turkey - this distinctive form shows a glossy jet-black head, contrasting strongly with the yellow throat.

▶ **Grey-headed Wagtail (***thunbergi)* rather uncommon, most frequent in spring on east coast, as birds head to northern Fenno-Scandinavia. Males show dark-grey head, darker-grey ear coverts. Sometimes a white moustachial stripe.

▲Most frequent continental form seen here (mainly in the south and east) is the **Blue-headed Wagtail.**

▶ **Sykes Wagtail** *(beema)* incredibly rare here, found on the Russian steppes. Reported every year - beautiful lavender-blue head with white supercilium, low ear covert and moustachial stripe, with a yellow throat. If seen, more likely to be a pale Blue-headed Wagtail.

▶ **Juveniles** (right) look washed out, but should show a yellow flush on the breast.

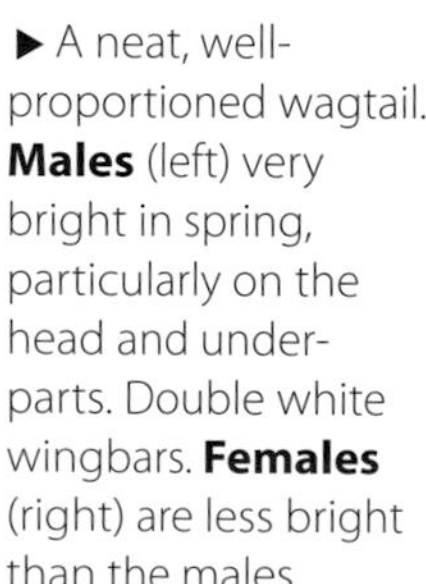

▶ A neat, well-proportioned wagtail. **Males** (left) very bright in spring, particularly on the head and under-parts. Double white wingbars. **Females** (right) are less bright than the males.

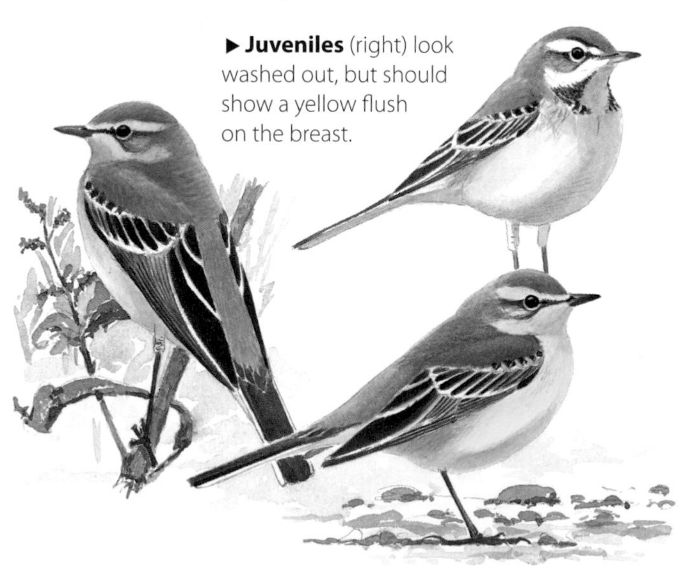

Grey Wagtail • *Motacilla cinerea*

17-20cm, 7in

When Throughout the year **Where** Breeds close to running water. Found around lakes, ponds and even city centres **Confusion species** Yellow Wagtail **Call** Distinctive, metallic *st-it* or *tzit*

A slim colourful bird, constantly on the move, dipping from rock to rock in search of food, with tail wagging.

▶ In flight, the long black and white tail will be obvious. Note the white wing bar and yellow rump, contrasting with darker upperpart colours.

◀ **Non breeding males** (top) lose the black throat and the breast becomes very pale. Females appear buff-white below. **Juvenile** (left) and first winter resemble the adults, but lack any colour on the throat. Buff supercilium, pinkish on the breast lacking the yellow shown by adults. Pinkish base to lower mandible, unlike the adults' black bill.

▶ **Females** lack the black throat patch and have less yellow on the breast.

▶ **Breeding males,** grey head and back contrasts with white face pattern, bordering an obvious black throat patch. Breast and vent are flushed strongly with yellow, fading to a paler yellow-white.

Pied Wagtail • *Motacilla alba*

16.5-19 cm, 7in

When Throughout the year. Coastal migrant in spring too (White Wagtail) **Where** From inner cities to coastal marshes. Big winter roosts can be found in rural and urban areas alike **Confusion species** Yellow and Grey Wagtail **Call** A high-pitched *chiz-zik or slee-vit*

◀ **Female** (right) in breeding plumage. Pied Wagtails are distinctive birds with striking black, grey and white plumage, a thin bill, a rather plump rounded body and long tail which they continually pump up and down. They are very approachable, almost brave little birds with no real fear of humans.

▶ **Juveniles** are grey- brown versions of adults. The face pattern appears a little more complex than those of the parents and, especially when recently fledged, they show a distinct creamy-yellow wash, occasionally inviting thoughts of a young Yellow Wagtail. The upperparts are a "dustier" grey tone compared to the adults with the pale yellowy wash extending across the wingbars too. Underparts tend be a little more buff than the adult birds, with a less striking blackish bib too. The striking grey flanks are much as the parents.

◀ **Continental White Wagtails** can often appear as markedly different than "our" Pied Wagtails, especially male Whites. They have distinctive silvery-toned pale grey upperparts and a "sharp" demarcation of the black on the nape and the pale grey mantle. Female White Wagtails are generally duller than the males, being much dingier looking birds but they still show a rather plain paler grey tone on the back, with less black on the head. Both sexes share a paler grey rump than the blackish tones shown by Pied Wagtail.

Richard's Pipit • *Anthus novaeseelandiae* 17-20cm,8in

When Mainly in autumn, rarer still in spring and winter **Where** Tends to favour grassy areas, mainly coastal, especially eastern counties **Confusion species** Tawny and Meadow Pipit **Call** A loud, resonant *schhreep,* or, occasionally, *cheep*

▲ In flight, distinctive pot belly and long tail always apparent, tends to undulate, closing wings as they go. Calls frequently in flight.

▶ Darker and more densely-streaked on the crown than Tawny Pipit. More obvious supercilium (with eye-ring effect) and pale lores. Beware of angle a bird may be standing in - can look dark.

◀ Pronounced malar stripe (all ages) heavily streaked breast. Bill stouter and pinker-based than Tawny Pipit (with streaked breast, resemble mini- thrushes). If seen on open ground, note very long hindclaw.

▶ Mantle dark and streaked on **adults** and juveniles. Wing coverts of adult are ginger- fringed, most juveniles show some brown on the median covert fringes.

Tawny Pipit • *Anthus campestris* 15.5-18cm, 7in

When Occasionally in late spring and early summer, more frequent in autumn **Where** Short turf areas (shorter areas than Richard's), dunes. Mainly coastal, southern England **Confusion species** Richard's and Meadow Pipit **Call** A short *chuup* or a longer *tsslhip*

Another large pipit, but, unlike Richard's, appears rather slim and invariably paler. Less long-legged, shorter-tailed and smaller-billed.

▶ **Juvenile** has heavy spotting on breast, and streaked mantle. More of a fringe than an edge to the dark coverts. Face pattern more pronounced with dark lores.

▶ **Breeding** adult pallid and plain (as non breeding), readily told from Richard's Pipit. Head finely streaked. Face plain, with dark line on lores. Upperparts plain sandy-grey, underparts fine streaks on breast sides, otherwise clean-looking. Wings show row of dark median coverts with whitish edges.

◀ Seen well, note fairly short hindclaw. Bill less stout than Richard's Pipit, with a darker-pink lower mandible.

Meadow Pipit • *Anthus pratensis*

14-15.5cm, 6in

When Throughout the year. Numbers rise in autumn **Where** Breeds in open country, also on moors, meadows and grassland. Migrants in spring and autumn **Confusion species** Other small pipits **Call** Commonest is a thin *tseep*

A small, streaked-brown pipit with a fine, thin bill and distinctive call. As well as brown versions, Meadow Pipits can look very grey, or olive, so beware! A greyish Meadow Pipit still retains the fairly heavy streaks on the breast and flanks. The bill looks quite thin and the head pattern is rather indistinct.

◀ During the breeding season, Meadow Pipits display with song flights. They take off with a few thin 'zeeps', then parachute down with a sweet song, ending with a flourishing trill.

▲ Fresh 'greenish' Meadow Pipits are rather neat, with bold mantle streaking and thin double white wing bars. Note the long-looking hind claw.

Juveniles resemble adults, but lack any obvious flank markings. Wing bars also appear neater than adult's.'Mipits' move through long grass with a very characteristic jerky action - a combination of furtiveness and running, which can make them look a little ungainly on occasion.

▲ **Adults at the** end of the breeding season (right) can have a moth- eaten, washed-out appearance. Face looks greyish-white and head and upperparts rather greyer than you might expect a Meadow Pipit to appear. Underparts look cleaner than at any other time of year. The strong suffusion of yellow- buff seen on autumn birds is absent and the birds look very white on the flanks.

Tree Pipit • *Anthus trivialis*

14-16cm, 6in

When Arrives from mid April onwards. Autumn migrants as well **Where** Open woodland, scrubby heaths, passage birds on coast **Confusion species** Meadow Pipit **Call** A fairly rasping *spheez*. Song is a lovely tzwee-zee-zee

Smallish, similar to Meadow Pipit but looks slightly bulkier and stealthier.

◀ In spring, **males'** song flight to attract females. Taking off from a perch, he begins singing, before parachuting with wings and tail spread, legs dangling to the same perch.

◀ Tree Pipit has heavier looking bill, bolder head pattern and thinner streaks on flanks than the Meadow Pipit. Wing bars are also often more distinct.

▲ **Males** also sing just below tree tops. They often pump their tail when on a branch.

Water Pipit • *Anthus spinoletta*

15.5-17cm, 6.5in

When Late autumn arrival. Some spring migrants from further afield **Where** Freshwater marshes, flooded fields (inland and coastal). Mainly south and east Britain **Confusion species** Rock and Meadow Pipit **Call** Similar to Rock Pipit but a softer-toned *veist*

Very similar to Rock Pipit, and, until the mid-1980s, were regarded as the same species.

▶ In flight, paler than Rock Pipit, with less heavily- marked under parts, paler face and distinctive white outer tail feathers.

▶ **Breeding adults** (left) dove-grey head with a bold white supercilium and throat, breast is flushed pink. Bill is less heavy than Rock Pipit, legs browner.

◀ **Non breeding adults** (right) cleaner than Rock Pipit. Head pattern is obvious, as are greyer upper- parts and neat breast streaks. Pale base to bill.

Rock Pipit • *Anthus petrosus*

15.5-17cm, 16.5in

When Found throughout the year, with migrants in spring and autumn **Where** Rocky coasts, especially on west coast and whole of Ireland. Scarce migrant of east coast **Confusion species** Meadow and Water Pipit **Call** An exploding *feest*

◀ In flight, from below Rock Pipit looks pretty dingy. Head and underparts look dark and the tail almost blackish, a hint of pale on the outer tail feathers. Song flight spring. During the winter and early spring, birds arriving from Scandinavia swell numbers of British Rock Pipits.These birds (of the race *littoralis)* resemble our Rock Pipits, but tend to look a little greyer around the head, with a rather well defined whitish, rather than indistinct buff, supercilium and also a blackish-looking bill. In spring, some Scandinavian Rock Pipits can resemble spring Water Pipits!

A sturdy-looking bird, appearing chunkier and darker than Meadow Pipit, with a noticeably longer bill.

▼ Very distinctive on the ground. Upperparts look almost oily in tone, the heavily-streaked underparts are rather sullied.The face pattern is minimal, a white eye-ring being the most obvious feature. Longish, dark bill and dark legs.The rear bird shows the important grey outer tail.

Waxwing • *Bombycilla garrulus*

18-21 cm, 8in

When Late October onwards, primarily midwinter **Where** Mainly north and east coasts, fond of berry bushes in housing estates and roadsides **Confusion species** None **Call** A delightful, gently-whistling *ssirrrr* reaching to a crescendo if many birds are in the flock

Rotund Starling-sized birds with distinctive plumage. Some winters, flocks of many hundreds arrive.The waxy red tips on secondaries are quite pronounced, lending the bird their name.

▶ **Females** (left) similar to **males** (right) but smaller, with a shorter crest and less defined bib. Waxy red tips and yellow tail band less obvious. Juveniles, browner with shorter crests.

▲ In flight, reminiscent of a slim Starling, with broad wings, shortish, square-tailed. Pale underwings, rufous vent and grey upperwings.

Dipper • *Cinclus cinclus*

17-20cm, 7in

When Year round. Migrants in autumn and winter **Where** Upland streams, rivers fast-flowing and rocky. Passage birds sometimes on mills and weirs **Confusion species** None **Call** Short, metallic *tzit*

A very distinctive, compact bird with unique aquatic habits. Found only by water, they bob up and down on rocks, before diving into the water.

▶ **Juveniles** soon pick up the parents' habits. They are scaly on the upperparts, with bold grey crescents on the breast and belly. Note short wings and tail.

▶ **Adults** have neat brown head, contrasting with big white breast bib and chestnut belly. Migrants from Europe have black-looking bellies. Dippers whizz along in flight, their short wings whirring as they go.

Dunnock • *Prunella modularis*

13-14.5cm, 5.5in

When Year round **Where** Scrubby cover, hedgerows, gardens in any situation **Confusion species** None **Call** Thin *teeh*. Song, resonant and rather melodic

▶ More slender, less dumpy bird than the House Sparrow and has a thinner bill, a longer tail and distinctly different plumage.

▲ Dunnocks have a delightful display to attract females. Landing on a small branch, a male will begin to flick one wing, then the next, in turn for several minutes. Often a lone male will quickly draw a crowd and will be joined by other like-minded wingflickers!

▲ **Juveniles** duller and far streakier than adult, head is much browner and the underparts are heavily blotched.

◀ **Adults are** warm-brown above with distinctive grey faces. Upper- and underparts are brown, streaked black. The sexes are similar, but males tend to be greyer on the head and throat.

Wren • *Troglodytes troglodytes*

9.5cm, 3.5in

When Throughout the year **Where** Woodland, scrub, farmland, reedbeds and (in the northern and western Isles of Scotland) on cliffs **Confusion species** None **Call** A rapid fire *cherr, cherr cherr,* or explosive, melodic trilling

Tiny birds with a stubby cocked tail and rich- brown plumage. Secretive in nature, furtively seeking food in tangled undergrowth; can be hard to see.

▶ In flight, often all that will be seen is a tiny brown bird whizzing by on whirring wings.

▲ Wrens are delicately-marked birds full of field marks. The rich-brown plumage is finely streaked above, with barred outer wing and buff-washed underparts.

▲ The stumpy tail is held cocked; note a bright yellow gape.

◀ The tiny rounded nests are tucked away in brambles or rock crevices. Males make several nests for females to choose from.

Robin • *Erithacus rubecula*

12.5–14cm, 5.5in

When Year round, migrants in autumn **Where** Woodland, scrubby areas, gardens and hedgerows. Migrants coastal **Confusion species** None **Call** A sharp, hard *tik*. Song a blend of excited, melodic tumbling notes

Plump, rotund, with a red breast and a lovely song, the Robin is one of our most recognizable species. They frequently sing in the winter proclaiming their territories early on. Aggressive birds, Robins will fight to maintain their status.

◀ A small, fat bird with, seemingly no neck, the most striking plumage feature is the bold orange-red face and breast, bordered by grey. Upperparts are contrastingly brown and the underparts are washed grey.

▲ **Juveniles** just as distinctive as adults. Head, upperparts and breast liberally speckled with dark brown spotting and scalloping. Red breasts from June-September.

Nightingale • *Luscinia megarhynchos*

15-16.5cm, 6in

When Arrives from early to mid-April. Passage birds in spring and autumn **Where** Breeds in open woodland and dense undergrowth, limited to south-east Britain. Passage birds on coast **Confusion species** None **Call** No real contact calls. Once heard, the song is never forgotten, a rich melody of whistles, trills and fluted notes

World famous for its incredible song, they are very hard to see and rather uninspiring too! Often sing throughout the night, but early morning and late evenings are best.

◀ **Juveniles** are scaly versions of the adults. Often well hidden, Large-looking 'liquid' eye and rufous undertail.

◀ A skulking bird, warm-brown upper- parts with a rich-brown rounded tail, underparts are suffused with sandy-buff.

Bluethroat • *Luscinia svecica* 13-14cm, 6in

When Some arrive in March and April (White-spotted), others later in spring (Red-spotted). Also seen in autumn **Where** Breeds in wet tussock areas and scrub. Passage birds mainly coastal **Confusion species** None **Call** Not heard often, mainly a hard *tchak*

Two distinct Bluethroat forms, White- and Red-spotted.

◀ In flight, note cold, grey-toned upperparts, with rusty-toned tail base and dark tail band.

▼ **Male 'White-spots'** have bold white central spot on electric-blue throat.

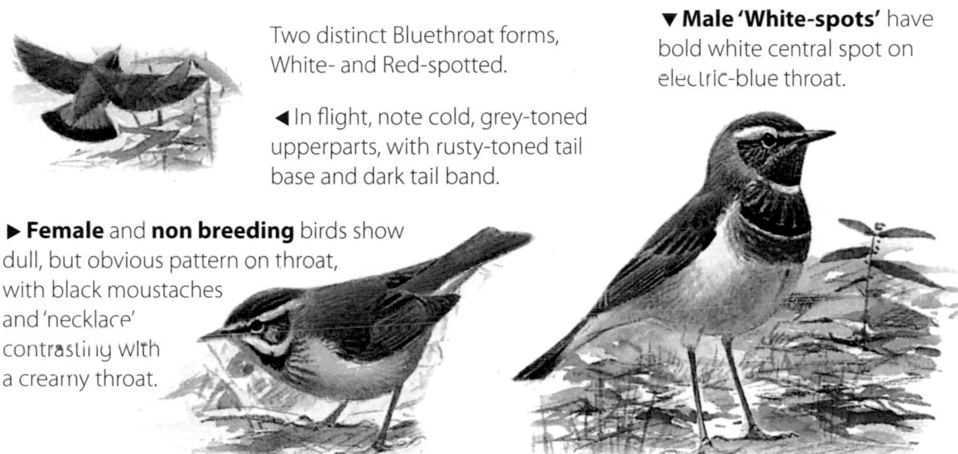

▶ **Female** and **non breeding** birds show dull, but obvious pattern on throat, with black moustaches and 'necklace' contrasting with a creamy throat.

Northern Wheatear • *Oenanthe oenanthe* 14-16.5cm, 6in

When Arrives from mid-March onwards, leaving in mid-autumn. Passage birds in spring and autumn **Where** Breeds in open, stony areas, often on moorland or farmland, but also on coastal sites. Migrants widespread on coasts **Confusion species** None **Call** A hard *chack*

◀ A plump bird, with nervous disposition: often flicks wings before flying. **Females** and juveniles lack dark mask. Browner upperparts than males.

▶ **Male** has distinctive gleaming white rump, black T-shape on tail and blue-grey upperparts.

◀ **Juveniles are** scaly, with bold ginger fringing on the closed wing.

▶ **Females** (left) brown above, with dark wings and buff-wash on breast. **Males** (right) have black mask, black wings, blue-grey upperparts and rich apricot breast.

Black Redstart • *Phoenicurus ochruros* 13-14.5cm, 5.5in

When Throughout the year, numbers rise with autumn migrants **Where** Breeds in towns and cities, on disused buildings, chimneys and factory roofs. Passage/wintering birds almost anywhere, mainly coasts **Confusion species** Common Redstart **Call** A hard sounding *tuk* or a whistled *wist*

A rather slim chat, with a habit of perching bolt upright and shivering its tail. Most frequently seen on autumn passage.

▶ **Males** jet-black face and upper breast contrasts with slate-grey upperparts and belly. Wings show a prominent white flash.

Females and juveniles are sooty-brown, except for darker wings and orange- . red tail. Fine black bill and button eye.

◀ **Non breeding male** resembles female, but is generally darker and greyer-looking. Tail can look very dark.

Common Redstart • *Phoenicurus phoenicurus* 14cm, 5.5in

When First birds arrive in mid-April, leaving in early autumn. Passage birds appear in September **Where** Breeds in deciduous or mixed woods. Passage birds mainly coastal **Confusion species** Black Redstart
Call A loud *huu-eet* and *tik-tik-tik*

Redstarts nest in natural holes or nest-boxes, or sometimes holes in walls.

◀ **Breeding males** spend much time in trees around the nest. The contrasting colour scheme unlike a male Black Redstart, with the face pattern and rich orange breast very striking.

▶ **Juvenile male** resembles female, but shows neater markings on the wings, and also has a mottled black face.

◀ **Females** brown above with orange wash on flanks. Warmer toned than female Black Redstart.

Whinchat • *Saxicola rubetra*

12-14cm, 5.5in

When Arrives from April onwards, last birds seen in October **Where** Breeds on open heath, rough pasture, moorland fringe. Coastal passage migrant **Confusion species** Stonechat **Call** A soft tec, tec

A short-tailed, plump bird, reminiscent of a Robin in shape and size. Frequently perch on fences and tops of vegetation. Habitually flicks wings and tail.

▶ In flight, **males** show white wing patches and tail sides. Note the distinctive head pattern.

▶ **Females** (left) and juveniles lack dark face of male. The duller underparts and head pattern separates them from Stonechat.

◀ **Males** (right) have very dark head, broken by broad white supercilium and moustachial stripe. Breast and flanks often a lovely deep ochre in colour.

Stonechat • *Saxicola torquata*

11.5-13cm, 5in

When Throughout the year. Birds seen on spring and autumn migration **Where** Breeds on heathland, moorland, banks of gorse. Passage/winter birds around coasts, fond of reedbeds **Confusion species** Whinchat **Call** Hard, loud *chak-chak*

Similar in size and habits to Whinchat.

◀ Moulting **juveniles** have broad fringing, and a hint of ochre on the breast.

◀ **Females are** brown-headed with dull orange breast and flanks. Dark streaks on mantle. Lacks bold supercilium of Whinchat.

▲ **Males** have bold white wing patches, dark head, and no white tail sides.

◀ **Breeding males** have black heads and obvious white neck patches. Also note the conspicuous white wing patch and rich orange breast and flanks.

Ring Ouzel • *Turdus torquatus*

24-27cm, 10in

When Birds arrive from March onwards. More frequent on spring passage than autumn **Where** Breeds around upland boulder slopes and gulleys. Passage birds like short-turfed areas **Confusion species** Blackbird **Call** Dry, clicking *tuc* or *tac*. Loud song, similar to Blackbird, but slower and more mournful

▶ **Breeding males** (left) have bold white crescent, scaled underparts and 'frosted' wings. Bill is yellow with dark tip, quite unlike Blackbird.

◀ **Females** (centre) are duller than first **winter males** (below right), often much browner in appear-ance. Underparts look quite scaled and the white crescent is less defined. Juveniles similar to Blackbirds, but with indistinct crescent and paler fringed upper- wing. Note scaling on underparts.

▲ In flight, the white crescent is obvious, note also paler-looking upper- and underwing.

Blackbird • *Turdus merula*

23.5-29cm, 10in

When Year round. Migrants in autumn **Where** Woods, parks, gardens across the country. Migrants on north and east coasts **Confusion species** Ring Ouzel **Call** Wide range of calls, *chink-chink* (often heard near dusk) and lovely, slow fluty song

◀ **Females** appear rufous or grey-brown, but vary. The throat is well marked, note the dull bare parts, similar to a juvenile.

◀ **Males** look glossy in summer, with bright yellow bill and eye ring.

▲ **Juveniles** appear more rufous than adult females and are more heavily mottled on both upper- and underparts. Throat and breast can look speckled, and thrush-like.

Mistle Thrush • *Turdus viscivorus*

22–27cm, 9–10.5in

When Throughout the year. Migrants in autumn **Where** Coniferous woods, parks, gardens and farmland across the country **Confusion species** Song Thrush **Call** A loud, wooden *zrtt-r-r-r-r* – like a football rattle

◀ In flight, note the white underwing, as well as the pale upperparts and boldly spotted underparts. Frequently call when flying.

▶ Can look rather 'pigeon-chested', especially when wings and tail are drooped. The bold spotting and cold grey upperparts are obvious; note the double wing bar.

▲ **Males** sing from top of tree. Song is similar to Blackbird, but more raucous, quicker and lacking a little melody.

▶ Large, boldly marked birds, with a long body and tail.

Song Thrush • *Turdus philomelos*

20-22cm, 9in

When Throughout the year **Where** Breeds in woodland and parks. Autumn migrants mainly on north and east coast **Confusion species** Mistle Thrush **Call** In flight, far carrying *tssip*. Alarm call is a loud *chuck-chuck*. Song is clear, languid and fluty, much mimicry and repeated phrases

◀ In flight, the spotting on the under-parts will be seen immediately. Check for the orange on the underwing.

◀ A gentle-looking bird, with brown upper- parts contrasting with yellow-washed, spotted underparts. There is a hint of a supercilium on the head, unlike Mistle Thrush.

▲ Smaller and more compact than Mistle Thrush. Breast is less boldly marked. Continental Song Thrushes stream into the country from September to November.

Fieldfare • *Turdus pilaris*

22-27cm, 9-10in

When Arrives from September, often lingers into April **Where** Hedges, copses, gardens anywhere. Breeds in small numbers in northern England and Scotland **Confusion species** Mistle Thrush **Call** Loud, chattering *chak, chak, chak*

◀ ▶ In flight, note the white underwing, while the grey rump, black tail and overall reddish hue are distinctive field points.

▼ Face on, the head and breast patterns contrast markedly while, from the side, the maroon back and wings contrast with the grey rump and back.

▲ Large, fairly bulky thrushes, reminiscent of Mistle Thrush in size and shape, but easily separated by plumage and call.

◀ In winter, commonly associate with other thrushes, particularly Redwings, forming large roving flocks, which quickly devour a berry-laden hedge or garden windfalls.

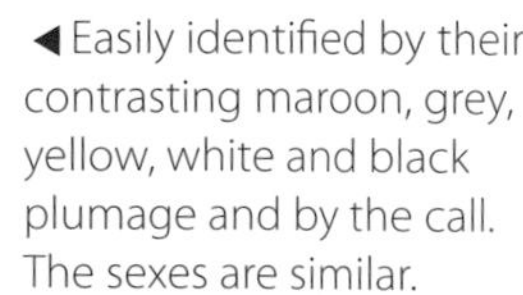

◀ Easily identified by their contrasting maroon, grey, yellow, white and black plumage and by the call. The sexes are similar.

Redwing • *Turdus iliacus*

19-23cm, 8-9in

When Arrives from mid-autumn, leaving in early spring **Where** Breeds in birch forests or bushes in northern Britain. Winter birds in berry trees, open fields or woodland **Confusion species** Song Thrush **Call** A thin, high pitched *tzzip*

▶ In flight, the most obvious feature seen is the red underwing and flanks. With a close view, the head pat-tern and streaked breast are also strik-ing. Often fly in disorderly flocks.

▲ Resembles Song Thrush, but is smaller and darker, with a distinctive face and underpart pattern.

▶ Redwings have a distinctive head pattern of a whitish supercilium and moustache, contrasting with brown head and upperparts. Underparts are white, with dark slender streaks extending to the flanks. Most obvious is the vibrant red flank patch, which extends onto the underwing.

◀ Very gregarious, feeds in flocks and the birds often bound and hop along the ground in synchrony.

Lesser Whitethroat • *Sylvia curruca*

11.5-13.5cm, 5in

When Arrives from late April to early May. Autumn birds into late September **Where** Breeds in hedgerows, dense scrub. Passage birds in coastal bushes. Absent in Scotland and Ireland **Confusion species** Common Whitethroat **Call** A dry *teck*. Song is drawn out series of rattling notes almost machine-gun-like!

A small, compact warbler with a fairly short tail.

▶ **Juveniles** appear greyer-around the head and back than juvenile Common Whitethroats, and show less rufous tones on the upperwing. Lesser always look slighter than Common Whitethroat

▶ **Adults** show a neat dark mask, con-trasting with the grey head. Upperparts are duller than Common Whitethroat, lacking any rufous tones on the wing. Underparts are white, with dingy flanks.

▲ In flight, looks fairly dark as it heads for cover, darker grey-brown than Common Whitethroat.The central tail feathers are blackish.

Common Whitethroat • *Sylvia communis*

13-15cm, 5.5in

When Appears in late April, leaves in September. Passage birds into October **Where** Breeds in scrub, open woodland, hedgerows, heathland **Confusion species** Lesser Whitethroat **Call** Most frequent is scolding alarm note *chur-ur*. Song short and fast scratchy warble

A chunky, sturdy warbler with long tail and cumbersome movements.

▶ **Males** show a gleaming white throat, contrasting with the grey head and pink, flushed under-parts. Dark tail with white outer feathers.

▶ **Females** look plain on the upper- parts except for a white eye ring and broad rufous fringes on the wings. Throat is still white.

▲ **Males** often announce their presence by song-flighting.

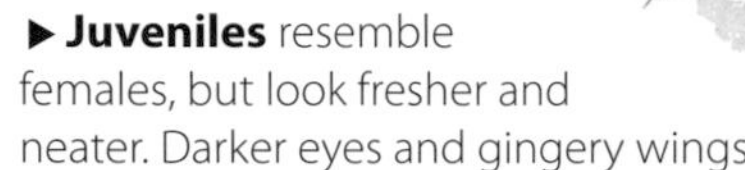

▶ **Juveniles** resemble females, but look fresher and neater. Darker eyes and gingery wings.

Blackcap • *Sylvia atricapilla*

13.5-15cm, 5.5in

When Year round **Where** Woods, copses, hedgerows across almost whole country. Winters in milder south and east **Confusion species** Garden Warbler **Call** A typical hard *teck* or toe. Song like a louder, more melodic Garden Warbler

◀ Not renowned for singing from treetops, preferring the cover of a hedge.

◀ **Females** have a rich russet-brown cap, a browner wash to the underparts, browner wings and a greyish-brown wash to the underparts.

A stockily-built warbler, roughly the same size as Garden Warbler, but looking a little longer and more slender in the body.

▲ **Males** show a glossy black cap, with silvery cheeks and nape. Upperparts are silvery-grey, darker on the wings and towards the tail tip.

Garden Warbler • *Sylvia borin*

13-14.5cm, 5.5in

When Arrives in mid- to late April. Seen into September **Where** Woodland, scrub, dense hedgerows and undergrowth. Absent in northern Scotland and much of Ireland **Confusion species** Barred Warbler, Blackcap **Call** Nasal *chek, chek*. Soft song, very like Blackcap, but a little quicker and longer

Rotund, plump bird, with rounded head, shortish tail and short stubby bill. Plain looking, can be very shy and retiring.

▶ The large eye and plain face give the Garden Warbler a gentle expression. The plumage is largely brown above, with a greyish suffusion on the face, and greyish-white below.

◀ **Juvenile** similar to adult, differing only in fresher plumage, browner upperparts and stronger buff wash on underparts. In the autumn can be confused with the much scarcer Barred Warbler.

Barred Warbler • *Sylvia nisoria*

15.5-17cm, 6.5in

When Very rare spring migrant, scarce autumn passage species. Appears from late August onwards, some arrive into November **Where** Coastal bushes, particularly elders and brambles. Mainly east coast **Confusion species** Garden Warbler (autumn only) **Call** A dry rattling *trrrrrutt*, rarely heard

A large, chunky warbler with a longish tail. No late summer is complete without one.

◀ In flight, be sure to look for white tail tips.

◀ **Juveniles** look fairly plain grey- brown with scaled upper- tail, flanks and undertail. The wings are well-marked with pale fringes and thin wing bars. Barred adults are incredibly rare. It is almost always juveniles that are seen.

Dartford Warbler • *Sylvia undata*

13-14cm, 5.5in

When Throughout the year. Rare migrant in spring and autumn **Where** Breeds on gorse-clad heathland, mainly southern and eastern England. Migrants coastal **Confusion species** None **Call** Harsh, scolding *chaiirr.* Song is a quick, rattled warble

A small bird, with plump body and long tail. Often fairly skulking, but males can become very obliging in early spring, when singing.

▶ **Males** proclaim their territory with lovely song flights, singing as they parachute down to another gorse bush.

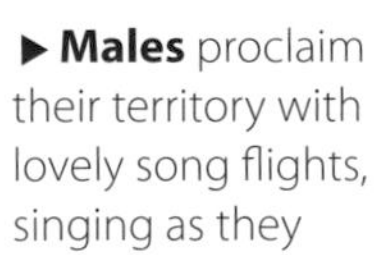

◀ **Females** are duller above, often tinged brownish and paler, rather dull, red wine-toned below.

▶ **Males** have entirely dark grey upperparts, contrasting with deep burgundy under-parts. Some white flecks are seen on throat. Tail is frequently held cocked. Note red orbital ring too.

Icterine Warbler • *Hippolais icterina* 12-13.5cm, 5in

When A few in spring, but mainly an autumn bird **Where** Scrub or copses around coasts, particularly along east coast **Confusion species** Melodious Warbler, Willow Warbler (autumn) **Call** Very rarely heard singing - a pleasing, loud, fast set of imitation and Kestrel like *kee-kee* notes

Tricky to identify, along with Melodious Warbler. Icterines are large-headed, long-winged birds, with stout bill and short, square tail.

▶ Spring males can look rather yellow and green.

▶ Plumage features are similar for both Icterine and Melodious Warblers. Note the distinct pale wing panel. Note the head pattern and, in particular, the long wings.

▶ Both Icterine and Melodious share similar head patterns - pale lores and short superciliums, but Icterine tend to show a more peaked crown. Icterine has grey-green upperparts in spring contrasting with yellow underparts. Spring birds show a distinct pale wing panel (lacking on Melodious).

Melodious Warbler • *Hippolais polyglotta* 12-13cm, 5in

When Mainly an early autumn species **Where** Scrubby coastal bushes, almost always on south coast and islands **Confusion species** Icterine Warbler, Willow Warblers (autumn) **Call** Rarely heard, but known to utter a sparrow-like chatter

Closely resembles an Icterine Warbler, but looks softer in the face, a little plumper and shorter winged.

▼ This bright Melodious Warbler shows similar plumage to an Icterine, but can be browner above and lacks a distinct wing panel. Bill is stouter and the primary projection is shorter too.

▶ Melodious Warbler appears more kindly than Icterine, with a less peaked crown. Spring birds very similar colour to Icterine, but the upperparts are often browner. Wings look rather plain (in autumn too), unlike Icterine. Note wing length - Melodious has a short primary projection, quite unlike Icterine. Melodious have brownish, not blue- looking, legs. Autumn birds are greyer, less yellow versions of spring birds - they still show no wing panel and dark legs.

Sedge Warbler • *Acrocephalus schoenobaenus* 12cm, 5in

When Arrives from early April onwards. Autumn birds into October **Where** Breeds in dense, damp vegetation around marshes. Passage birds in coastal scrub **Confusion species** Reed Warbler (singing only), Aquatic Warbler (juveniles only) **Call** Hard *tsek*. Song very like Reed Warbler, full of trills and flourishes. Throws in more variation, unlike Reed Warbler

◀ Medium-sized with a distinctive head pattern and neat song flight in spring. **Adults** have a bold white supercilium and throat, with dark crown and cheeks. Upperparts heavily streaked, but rufous rump is plain. Males dis-play flight almost as soon as they arrive, unlike the Reed Warbler.

◀ **Juveniles** show a streaked breast, yellow upperparts and a buff central crown stripe.

Aquatic Warbler • *Acrocephalus paludicola* 11.5-13cm, 5in

When Appears from early August into October **Where** Low areas of sedge, reedbed fringe. Almost entirely in southwest England. Very rare elsewhere **Confusion species** Sedge Warbler **Call** Rarely heard, a low *chack*

◀ **Adults** and juveniles share striking head pattern and yellow-ochre tones, compared to Sedge Warbler. Both have broad buff-yellow mantle braces, with blackish borders. With a really good view, check rump for the streaks typical of Aquatic Warbler. Hard birds to get to grips with, good views are needed to ensure identification is right.

▲ Adults' head pattern is distinctive. **Juveniles** look rather black and yellow. Note broad straw-yellow supercilium and narrower median-crown stripe, narrow black eyestripe and border to crown. Also, note the unmarked breast, unlike juvenile Sedge Warbler.

Reed Warbler • *Acrocephalus scirpaceus* 12.5cm, 5in

When Arrives late April/early May onwards. Migrants through to October **Where** Breeds in reedbeds and in other vegetation in damp areas. Migrants in scrub and coastal bushes **Confusion species** Marsh Warbler **Call** Short, hard *chet*

A rather plain-looking bird, slimmer than Sedge Warbler with a flattish-looking forehead and long, thin bill.

▶ Reed Warblers have short superciliums, quite unlike Sedge Warbler. Upperparts are plain sandy-brown with a warmer-tone to the rump. Underparts are white, with buff flanks. Long, thin bill unlike the stumpy bill of Sedge Warbler.

▲ Often sings from exposed reed stems. Song is similar to Sedge Warbler, but tends to sound dryer, a little more scratchy and a bit monotonous.

Marsh Warbler • *Acrocephalus palustris* 13-15cm, 5-6in

When Arrives from May onwards **Where** Vegetated ditches and damp meadows in southern England. Migrants coastal, mainly east coast **Confusion species** Reed Warbler **Call** Similar to Reed Warbler. Song quite different, high-pitched, fast mix of notes, with much mimicry from other species

Very like Reed Warbler, and best identified by song (and occasionally habitat) alone.

▶ Slightly shorter bill and more rounded head than Reed Warbler. Plumage also tends to appear a little greyer-green above and the rump perhaps a little less rufous. Flanks show a pale-yellow suffusion. With autumn birds, look for pale tips to the primaries and yellow legs but be cautious when identifying.

Grasshopper Warbler • *Locustella naevia*

12.5–13.5cm, 5in

When Arrives from April, with passage birds in autumn **Where** Nests in low, damp vegetation and open scrub. Passage birds mainly coastal **Confusion species** Savi's Warbler **Call** Males sing for hours - a dry, mechanical reeling in long bursts of a minute or two. They get louder/quieter as the bird moves its head

▲ A fairly secretive, small to medium-sized warbler with few plumage features and a striking song.

▶ A Best views at dawn and dusk when they are likely to be singing. The head is rather plain, but the mantle and wings are streaked. Flanks are washed buff, note the streaked or spotted undertail.

Cetti's Warbler • *Cettia cetti*

13-14cm, 5in

When Throughout the year **Where** Breeds in tall, dense cover near lakes and reedbeds. Mainly in southern England, some in East Anglia **Confusion species** Reed Warbler **Call** Loud, ringing *pliit*. Song explosive, melodic set of variable notes *chip-cheewit-witchitt*

A stocky, medium-sized warbler, very tricky to see, as they skulk in thick vegetation.

▶ Richly-coloured birds, with an off-white supercilium and whitish throat, contrasting with buff-grey underparts. Note the broad tail and shortish wings. Listen out for the incredible song!

Goldcrest • *Regulus regulus*

8.5–9.5cm, 3.5in

When Year round **Where** Woods (especially coniferous forests), dense cover and bushes around country. Autumn birds on north and east coast **Confusion species** Firecrest, Pallas's and Yellow-browed Warbler **Call** A high-pitched zee-zee-zee-zee-zee. Song a repeated squeaky *peet-ee-liu*

Smallest bird in Europe Agile birds flicking constantly for aphids or flycatching. When not moving through treetops, equally at home 'foraging' through small bushes and grass.

▶ **Males** have rich-red centres to the crown feathers, contrasting with the black borders and greenish upperparts. The wings are strikingly black and white, with a short dark, notched tail.

◀ **Females** basically resemble the male, except for a bright yellow crown stripe.

Firecrest • *Regulus ignicapillus*

9-10cm, 3.5in

When Mainly in spring (especially April) and autumn (September/October) **Where** Breeds in mixed or deciduous woodland. Migrants in woods, scrub, mainly coastal in south and east **Confusion species** Goldcrest **Call** A strident zeeet, lower in tone than Goldcrest

▶ **Juveniles** lack bold patterning, just a white supercilium is seen. Wing bars also less defined.

A tiny, active bird, almost identical in size and structure to Goldcrest, but perhaps a tad chunkier.

◀ **Males** have a flame-coloured central stripe. Green mantle. Underparts white, buff breast sides. Note the bold, white supercilium.

◀ **Females** have a yellow central crown stripe, not as bright on mantle and wings.

Pallas's Warbler • *Phylloscopus proregulus*

9-9.5cm, 3.5in

When Almost always arrives in October, some linger into early winter **Where** Copses, bushes and hedges along coast. Mainly Northern Isles and east coast **Confusion species** Yellow-browed Warbler, Goldcrest **Call** Soft, quiet *chew-ee*

Pallas's Warbler is a tiny jewel of a bird, barely the size of a Goldcrest and constantly on the move.

▶ Not as hefty as Yellow-browed Warbler, and has a markedly different head pattern and a lemon yellow rump patch too. The bill is stubbier and darker than Yellow-browed Warbler. Pallas's Warbler often hovers on the outside of a bush when feeding.

Yellow-browed Warbler • *Phylloscopus inornatus*

9.5cm, 4in

When Mainly autumn, from September to November. Occasional wintering records **Where** Wooded coastal locations, also in scrub, hedges. Found from Northern Isles down east coast to southwest England **Confusion species** Pallas's Warbler, Goldcrest **Call** Often the first thing that alerts you to one, a Coal Tit-like *tssooeet* or *sweet*

Small birds that arrive here from Siberian taiga forests. Smaller and plumper than Chiffchaffs, they are very active.

◀ Generally very clean-looking birds, note the Yellow-browed Warbler's wingbars and broad tertial edges. The head pattern is very distinctive too, as are the dazzling white underparts.

Wood Warbler • *Phylloscopus sibilatrix*

11-12.5cm, 4.5in

When Arrives in mid-April, leaving by August. More frequent spring passage bird, scarce in autumn. Rare in Ireland **Where** Mature deciduous woodland, with plenty of canopy shade. Passage birds are coastal **Confusion species** Willow Warbler, Chiffchaff **Call** A hard *ziip* or *pee-uo*. Song resembles a coin spun on a metal plate, an accelerating trill

▶ Wood Warblers often sing from a shaded branch where they have a view of what's going on around them. Singing birds quiver from bill tip to tail tip when in full flow.

▼ A smallish bird appearing broad-chested and short-tailed, much more so than its confusion species. Often you will catch a view of a Wood Warbler from below only. They look far broader in the chest than other members of the *Phylloscopus* group (Chiffchaff & Willow Warbler). The shortness of the tail is very noticeable too. The clean white look to the underparts is also something of a give away, contrasting starkly with the bright lemon throat.

▲ **Juveniles** look duller than adults, but remain far cleaner above and below than either Willow Warbler or Chiffchaff.

Chiffchaff • *Phylloscopus collybita*

10-12cm, 4–4.5in

When Throughout the year **Where** Any type of woodland in spring. Countrywide **Confusion species** Willow Warbler **Call** A plaintive *hueet*. Song a repetitive *chiff-if-chaff*, heard from late winter onwards

▲ In spring 'Chiffys' move quickly through cover, constantly flicking wings and jerking from branch to branch.

▼ Slightly smaller than Willow Warbler, with a more rounded head, shorter wings and more stocky appearance. In autumn, British populations are bolstered by birds from Scandinavia and Siberia. These birds are generally greyer-brown than the more olive-brown individuals normally seen.

▶ Note the greyish-white supercilium, blackish eye-stripe and pale-looking ear coverts. Upperparts are generally olive-green, with darker wings. Underparts are buff-white except for a white throat. Darkish, thin bill. Legs are dark brown, unlike Willow Warbler.

Willow Warbler • *Phylloscopus trochilus* 11-12.5cm, 4–5in

When Early spring arrival, leaving throughout the autumn **Where** Young trees, bushes, woodland fringe across the whole country **Confusion species** Chiffchaff **Call** Similar to Chiffchaff, a more penetrating *hoo-eat*. Song descending set of flourishing notes

▶ Very similar to the stockier Chiffchaff. Note the long wing length (short on Chiffchaff) and the leg colour (pale on Willow Warbler, dark on Chiffchaff).

▲ **Autumn birds** closely resemble spring birds but may look more yellowy below.

▼ **Spring birds** generally paler than Chiffchaffs. Head and upperparts have a yellow-tinged, long supercilium, not short and buff like Chiffchaff. A pencil-thin black eye-stripe and slightly blotched cheeks are also apparent. Underparts are cleaner than the Chiffchaff's, lacking buff tones. Bill shows a dark upper mandible and tip, with a flesh-pink lower mandible.

▲ **Juveniles** in autumn can be striking. Upperparts are pale olive-green, with rich lemon underparts

Spotted Flycatcher • *Muscicapa striata* 13.5-15cm, 5.5in

When Arrives from mid-May, leaving in late September **Where** Parkland, open woodland, gardens across entire region, except north-west Ireland **Confusion species** Pied Flycatcher (females and autumn birds only) **Call** A thin *tzee*. Song is made up of several wheezy notes

▼**Juveniles** heavily-scalloped head, mantle and breast, contrasting with the broadly- fringed grey-brown wings and dark tail.

▲In flight, very acrobatic as they catch assorted flying insects - including bees, butterflies and greenfly. They twist and turn, close to the ground, before returning to the same twig or branch.

▶A sparrow-sized bird with long wings, a squarish tail, short legs, big eyes and a broad-based bill.

◀**Adults** have grey-brown upperparts, with some dark streaking on the head. Darker wings, note the indistinct white bars. Underparts show streaking on the throat and breast. Dark tail has white outer feathers.

Pied Flycatcher • *Ficedula hypoleuca* 12-13.5cm, 4.5-5in

When Arrives from mid-April onwards, passage birds into June and then in autumn **Where** Breeds in deciduous woodland in western Britain, Wales and Scotland. Passage birds on coast **Confusion species** Spotted Flycatcher (autumn only) **Call** A sharp *tik, tik.* Song repeated *ree-zi, ree-zi*, with trills

▶ **Females** and **juveniles** can resemble Spotted Flycatchers in autumn, brown above, whitish below. Size and white wing flashes separate the two.

▲ Make frequent feeding sallies from the canopy. Note bold white wing patches on **male.**

Smaller and more rotund than Spotted Flycatcher. Breeding and passage birds always seem nervous and active.

◀ **Males** are unmistakable. The contrasting black and white can be seen from a distance. Note the large wing flash and white patch above bill.

Red-breasted Flycatcher • *Ficedula parva* 11–12cm, 4.5in

When Very occasionally in spring (May), more frequent in autumn **Where** Almost always coastal, in copses, bushes and low cover **Confusion species** Other flycatchers (autumn only) **Call** A soft, Wren-like *seerrt*

Small, with a rounded head and body; frequently cocks its longish tail.

▶ In flight, note the contrasting upperparts and Wheatear-like tail pattern, white sides with inverted black T-shape.

▲ **Females** (above) and juveniles look brownish on the head, and lack the red on the breast. They have a distinctive narrow white eye-ring.

◀ **Breeding males** are rare in UK, but have been seen here in both spring and autumn. Note the grey wash to the face, contrasting with the brown upperparts.

Blue Tit • *Parus caeruleus*

10.5-12cm, 5in

When Throughout the year **Where** Woodland, hedges, gardens in any situation across country **Confusion species** None **Call** A cheeky, harsh *churr-urr-urr*

Small birds with rounded heads and, seemingly, no shoulders. Frequent visitors to gardens. Like many members of the family, will flock in winter. Loves feeding on peanuts or coconuts hung in gardens or on windows.

▶ **Juveniles are** yellow, green and black, duller than adults. Will sit close together after fledging. No trace of white like adults.

◀ **Adults** have sky-blue crowns. Mantle and rump are lime-green, notched tail blue-grey. The wings are sky-blue with a thin white wing bar. Has a black central streak on belly.

Great Tit • *Parus major*

13.5-15cm, 5.5in

When Throughout the year **Where** Woodland, parks, gardens, even reedbeds across the country **Confusion species** None **Call** A loud, resonant *teecha-teecha- teecha* and a ringing *zinc, zinc*

Largest member of the family seen in Britain and Ireland. Almost House Sparrow size. Can be rather aggressive.

▼ **Juveniles** look washed-out compared to adults. Plumage is subdued, with yellow on the cheeks and underparts. Breast stripe is indistinct.

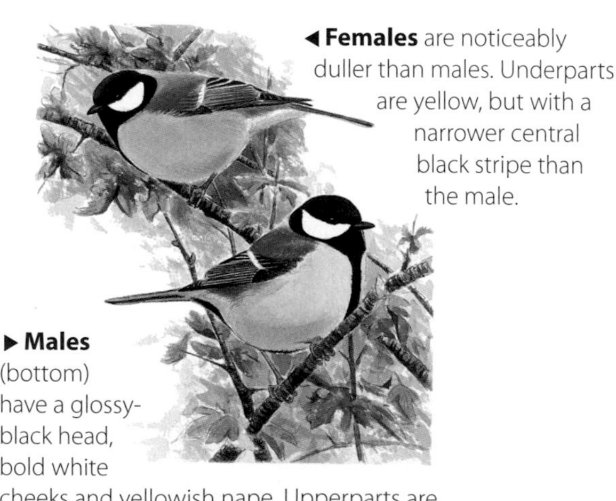

◀ **Females** are noticeably duller than males. Underparts are yellow, but with a narrower central black stripe than the male.

▶ **Males** (bottom) have a glossy-black head, bold white cheeks and yellowish nape. Upperparts are brighter olive than the female. The belly is bright yellow, with a broad black central band.

Crested Tit • *Parus cristatus*

10.5–12cm, 4–4.5in

When Year round **Where** Confined to the Caledonian forests of the Scottish Highlands **Confusion species** None **Call** Most frequent is a buzzing *buurrrret*

A smallish member of the family which can be tricky to find. Equally though, they can be really inquisitive and approach to within touching distance.

▶ They are frequently seen feeding in native pines, searching for food, where they adopt familiar tit family postures.

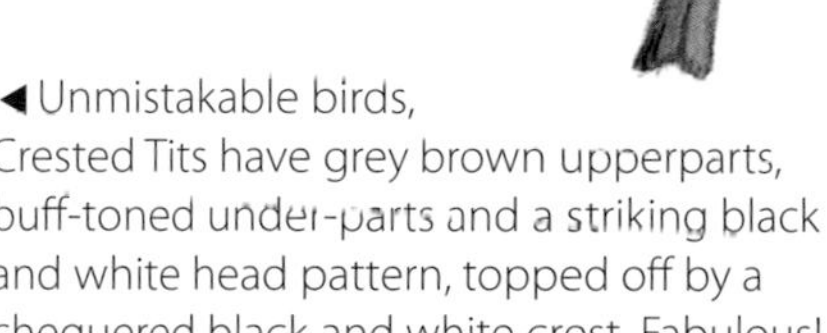

◀ Unmistakable birds, Crested Tits have grey brown upperparts, buff-toned under-parts and a striking black and white head pattern, topped off by a chequered black and white crest. Fabulous!

Coal Tit • *Parus ater*

10.5–11cm, 4in

When Year round, autumn migrant **Where** Countrywide, mainly coniferous woodland, but deciduous too. Also hedges and gardens **Confusion species** None **Call** A thin *tseu*. Song a distinctive *pitchou, pitchou, pitchou*

◀ **Juveniles'** patterns similar to adults, but the colours more subdued and appear rather yellow all over.

▶ **Irish birds** have a yellowy wash to the nape and cheeks; the upperparts are buff in tone.

▶ **Adults** have glossy black crowns and bibs, with bold white cheeks and rear nape patch. Upperparts olive-grey, white wing bars prominent. Below the bib is a small white patch on upper breast. Continental migrants from northern Europe differ from British birds - whiter cheeks, greyer back and paler buff-pink underparts.

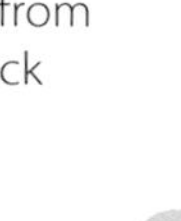

Marsh Tit • *Parus palustris*

11.5-13cm, 4.5-5in

When Year round **Where** Damp, broadleaf woods, parks and some gardens. Absent from Ireland and most of Scotland **Confusion species** Willow Tit **Call** A nasal *pitchou or pitchou ke-ke-ke*

A thick neck, stubby bill and round head. Very similar to Willow Tit.The wings look plain, lacking a wing panel, which Willow Tit does show.

▲ Glossy-looking cap, extending to the rear nape. White cheeks, fading to buff behind the ear coverts. Small black bib on the chin.

▶ Frequent users of nest holes, but, unlike Willow Tit, they do not excavate their own holes, preferring to make use of natural cavities.

◀ In early months of the year, a Marsh Tit will be pristine and can resemble Willow Tit. The wing of Marsh may show pale edges, but always less obvious than a spring Willow Tit.

Willow Tit • *Parus montanus*

12-13cm, 5in

When Throughout the year **Where** Damp woodland, especially alder and birch scrub. Absent from Ireland and most of Scotland **Confusion species** Marsh Tit **Call** A loud, deep, buzzy *tchav-tchav-tchav*

Rounded birds with particularly thickset appearance. Large head and 'bullneck' can be a distinctive feature.

◀ Willow Tits nest in holes which they tend to excavate themselves in rotten tree stumps.

▲ Dull, sooty crown apparent. The black bib will always be larger and broader on Willow Tit.

▲ The slightly rounded tail has paler outer tail feathers than Marsh Tit.

▶ Dull black cap extending to the mantle. Cheeks are all-white (not white and buff as on Marsh Tit) and, as mentioned above, the bib on chin is larger. Fresh plumaged birds have a distinctive pale wing panel, generally lacking on Marsh Tits.

Long-tailed Tit • *Aegithalos caudatus* 13-15cm, 5-6in

When Year round **Where** Woodland, scrub, hedgerows across Britain, except northern most Scotland. Absent from Ireland **Confusion species** None **Call** A piercing *tsee, tsee, tsee*

The tiny oval body, rounded head, short stubby bill, distinctive plumage and massively long tail make this species unmistakable.

▲ Long-tails don't eat as many seeds as other tits, preferring to eat insects. Highly agile in their search for food amongst leaves and twigs, they hang upside down by one foot while clutching food in the other.

▶ A delicate oval-shaped nest made of spiders' webs, moss, lichens and lined with feathers.

▶ Whitish heads with two broad black bands running from the bill base to the nape. Wings show pink scapulars and broad white edges to the tertials. Underparts are off-white, with a pink flush to the flanks and belly. The long tail is black with white outer feathers, spotted white on black from below.

Bearded Tit • *Panurus biarmicus*

14-15.5cm, 5.5in

When Can be seen year round, with birds moving in autumn in mini irruptions **Where** Breeds entirely in reedbeds, mainly along the east and south coast **Confusion species** None **Call** Twangy *piing-piing*

This is a rather plump-bodied, smallish headed but very long-tailed bird which isn't a tit at all! They are actually babblers, with their closest relatives living in Asia and Africa. Many birdwatchers refer to them as Bearded Reedlings.

▶ A typical view of a flock of Bearded Tits - a flurry of whirring wings and orange and grey exploding noisily out of reedbed. In autumn, flocks of 'Beardies' can often be seen, in sizeable flocks, towering up high in the sky and heading away in to the sky.

▼ **Juveniles** (right) have striking black backs and tail sides. Young Bearded Tits generally look a little less bright in overall plumage tone than the adults (especially the males). A good view will also show the neat little "mini-mask" in front of the eyes (on the lores). Juvenile male Bearded Tits have piercing white eyes, young females darker, but both sexes become paler as they grow. Bearded Tits can have as many as three broods in a good summer.

▼ **Males** (centre) are a truly handsome bird! They have striking dove-grey head contrasting with deep black moustachial stripes and a white throat. Upperparts are a rich, deep orange and they too contrast with the black and white markings on the wings. Underparts look much paler than upperparts, look too for the black area under the tail. Bearded Tits feed by picking insects off reedstems or, in autumn and winter, taking seeds from the reedbed floor.

▶ **Females** (left) are a more subdued version of the male, lacking the distinctive head pattern and those bold black moustachial stripes. They are also less rich in tone than the rich orangey males, but are still very distinctive. Look for the plain faced look and the orangey head.

Nuthatch • *Sitta europaea*

12-14.5cm, 4.5-5.5in

When Throughout the year **Where** Deciduous, mature woodland or parkland. Found south of a line running from the Solway to the Tees. Absent from Ireland **Confusion species** Lesser Spotted Woodpecker (flight only) **Call** A loud, full-sounding *chewit-chewit*

▲ Flight is undulating and, along with the size and shape, gives an initial impression of a small woodpecker. A good view will reveal the grey upper- parts and buff-orange underparts.

▲ **Males** have chestnut flanks, paler on the female. Bill is blackish, with a silvery base.

◀ A compact, torpedo-shaped body, short tail and hefty sharp- looking bill, reminiscent of a blue-grey woodpecker. Juveniles have brown tinged upperparts, a narrower, duller mask and dull brown flanks.

▼ Steely blue-grey upperparts and wings, with black and white tail sides. Note the broad black eye-stripe, contrasting with the white throat. Nuthatches are equally at home foraging in leaf litter or grass.

Common Treecreeper • *Certhia familiaris*

12.5-14cm, 5in

When Throughout the year **Where** Woodland, parks and gardens across the country **Confusion species** None **Call** A high-pitched, thin *tsee*

Small, almost mouse-like, with a short, decurved bill, beautifully camouflaged plumage and somewhat elusive habits.

◀ Undulating flight, note buff and black wing bars, rufous rump and notched tail.

▼ **Adults** find food by moving up and around the trunk and branches, picking up insects from bark crevices, before dropping to the bottom of another tree and starting the process again.

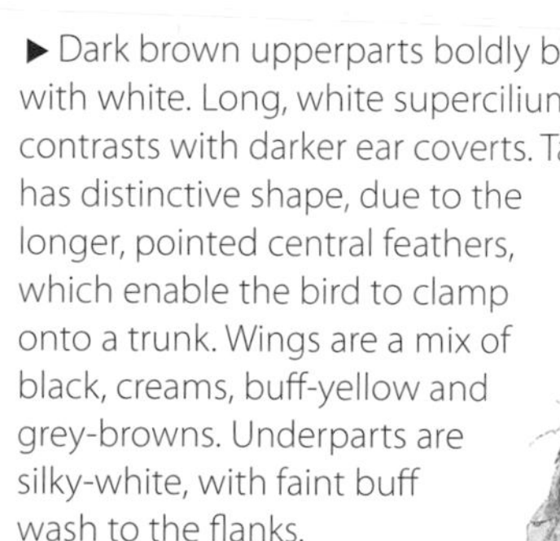

▶ Dark brown upperparts boldly blotched with white. Long, white supercilium contrasts with darker ear coverts. Tail has distinctive shape, due to the longer, pointed central feathers, which enable the bird to clamp onto a trunk. Wings are a mix of black, creams, buff-yellow and grey-browns. Underparts are silky-white, with faint buff wash to the flanks.

Golden Oriole • *Oriolus oriolus*

22–25cm, 8.5–9.5in

When Arrives from mid-April onwards. Passage birds into June, occasionally in autumn **Where** Former breeder in East Anglian poplar plantations. Passage birds mainly coastal, in copses **Confusion species** Green Woodpecker **Call** Harsh Jay-like *yeeaahk*. Song a loud, beautiful, fluted whistle

◀ Gentle undulating woodpecker-like flight.

▼ **Males'** (right) colours and song amazing. Slightly larger than a Starling, but different in shape. Dazzling rich golden head and body contrasts with jet-black wings and golden tipped black tail. Bill is rich-red.

▶ **Females (left) and juveniles** reminiscent of Green Woodpeckers in colour, but shape is different. Upperparts generally pale lime-green, with darker wings. Underparts off-white with fine dark streaks on breast. Bill is a dull red-brown.

Woodchat Shrike • *Lanius senator*

17-19cm, 7.5in

When Mainly spring, from April onwards, also early to mid-autumn **Where** Hedgerows, bushes, fences, mainly coastal, especially southern counties **Confusion species** Red-backed Shrike (non breeding birds only) **Call** A dry and grating rattle

Hooked bill, rounded head and body and long tail. Appears slightly chunkier than Red-backed Shrike. Adults are unmistakable.

▶ **Male,** dark-russet crown, black mask and pale loral spot. Mantle and wings black, with white scapular patch, white patch on primaries. Rump greyish white, with black tail (white outer tail feathers). Underparts white, washed buff on breast sides. Females crown more orangey, greyer on mantle. Often pale vermiculations on breast and flanks, whiter loral patch.

▶ **Juveniles** heavily-scaled. Brown mask, dark-scaled, grey head, pale throat and underparts. Mantle buff-brown, with white/black scales. Wings variegated, with black/white scapulars and coverts, ginger and black remainder. Note buff patch at base of primaries. Bill silver-grey with darker tip.

Red-backed Shrike • *Lanius collurio*

16-18cm, 7in

When Appears from May in spring, and from August in autumn **Where** Very irregular breeding species, now favouring scrubby heathland. Passage birds in coastal hedgerows and scrub **Confusion species** Other brown shrikes (autumn only) **Call** Rarely heard

Rare sporadic breeding bird, a sad demise for a once common breeding species. Medium-sized, with a rounded head and body, as well as a longish tail.

▶ **Males** are distinctive. Grey head, black mask and white throat. Upperparts are deep reddish-brown, flushed pink on underparts. Tail pattern has white sides with very thick, black inverted T-shape.

◀ **Females** are brown backed, with a hint of grey on nape only. Underparts are rather scaly.

▶ **Juveniles** are even more scaly, especially on the back. All have darkish hooked bills.

Great Grey Shrike • *Lanius excubitor*

22-26cm, 11 in

When Occasionally in early spring, most birds in autumn. A few winter at traditional spots **Where** Migrants mainly seen along east coasts. Wintering birds on large open heaths or moorland fringe **Confusion species** None **Call** Generally silent

A large member of the family, clearly larger than Red-backed, with distinctive plumage and habits.

▼ **Juveniles/first-winters** (right) less frequently seen. Duller than adults, with less prominent white marks on the wings, a less obvious mask, scalier under-parts and a pale-based bill.

▶ **Adults** have bold grey, white and black markings. Tail often waved up and down when perched. Note small, hooked bill.

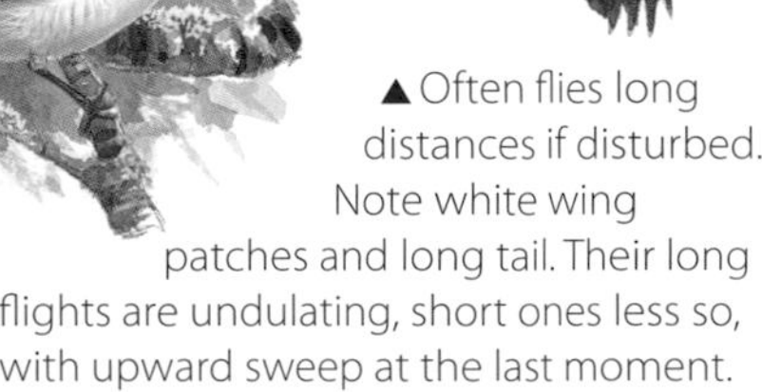

▲ Often flies long distances if disturbed. Note white wing patches and long tail. Their long flights are undulating, short ones less so, with upward sweep at the last moment.

Starling • *Sturnus vulgaris*

19-22cm, 9in

When Year round **Where** Farmland, cliffs, towns and cities across the country. Passage birds in autumn **Confusion species** None **Call** A hard *chuurrr.* Amazing mimic when singing, including a variety of other birds

Slightly smaller than Song Thrush, with a slim, pointed bill and peaked forehead. Many hundreds of thousands of birds from northern and eastern Europe move westwards in the late summer and into the autumn.

▲▼ Autumn and winter flocks are a common sight over cities, towns and in the countryside.

▲ **Juveniles** are wholly buff-grey-brown, except for a whitish throat and greyish mottling on the underparts.

▲ When they begin moulting to their **first-winter plumage,** juveniles can look quite odd in a 'half and half transitional plumage.

▼ Starlings appear blackish, but close views show the head and entire underparts have a distinctive purple iridescent gloss to the breast, fading to bottle- green on the flanks. The upper-parts are also very dark, with fine flecks on the mantle, rump and wings. **Males** show fewer spots compared to females.

Chough • *Pyrrhocorrax pyrrhocorrax*

37-41 cm, 16in

When Throughout the year. Migrants appear in early spring and winter **Where** Breeds around rocky cliffs, adjacent open farmland, in western Britain, Scotland and Ireland **Confusion species** Other crows **Call** A loud, strident *chioaw*

◀ In flight, note the 'fingered' look to the wings, and the short, broad-based tail.

▶ Seen well, the Chough is a fairly unmistakable, slim Jackdaw-sized crow. Often seen in small roving flocks, especially outside of the breeding season.

▼ Neatly-proportioned, glossy, black birds, with obvious decurved red bills and duller red legs. Juveniles have yellower bills.

Magpie • *Pica pica*

40-51 cm, 16–20in

When Throughout the year **Where** Woods, hedges, coastal bushes and moorland in all but northern Scotland **Confusion species** None **Call** A loud, chattering *chacka,* also hoarse *tzsee-tzsee-tzsee*

◀ A distinctive member of the crow family. Their black, white and iridescent plumage, chunky, stout bill and long black tail make Magpies unmistakable.

▼ Magpies fly with a combination of quick beats interspersed by glides. The white flight feathers and the prominent white V-shape on the back contrast with the dark plumage. Note long, tapered tail.

▲ **Juveniles are** very similar to adults.

▲ **Newly fledged** Magpies look a picture of innocence. Youngsters can stay quiet for long periods of time, waiting for adults to bring them food.

◀ Magpies have entirely jet-black upperparts and breast. The belly is bright white, contrasting with the black undertail. Note the bold white scapular patch. The long tail has a gleaming iridescence, green turning to blue at the tip.

Jay • *Garrulus glandarius*

33-36cm, 13-14in

When Throughout the year **Where** Woodland fringes, plantations and parkland. Absent from northern Scotland and south-west Ireland **Confusion species** Hoopoe **Call** A loud, harsh *kraa*

Chunky, rather elusive birds with a stout, heavy bill and colourful plumage.

◀ Pink, black, white and blue merge as they fly - a slow, deliberate, undulating flight.

▶ In autumn, Jays congregate in small groups to collect and store nuts for winter. They hop clumsily, burying their food.

▲ Mainly pinkish-buff all over, with a streaked crown and distinctive face. Mantle and upper half of the closed wing are brownish-pink, with a beautiful aquamarine 'elbow', notched black and white. Rump is snowy-white and the longish tail is black.

Jackdaw • *Corvus monedula*

30-34cm, 13in

When Throughout the year. Occasional migrant **Where** Woods, cliffs, towns and cities across the country **Confusion species** Carrion Crow, Rook **Call** Strident *keyaa and ky-aack*

Short-billed, compact member of the crow family. When identifying crows, check the size, bill colour and shape, and plumage detail.

▲ Roosts look spectacular. Birds can drop like a stone out of a flock, and more will follow in a remarkably agile aerial display.

▶ The head shows a glossy black cap and bib, contrasting strongly with a pale grey nape. Upperparts are sooty-black with, in certain lights, a strong green-purple gloss, particularly on the wings. Underparts are dark grey. Note the white eye and short, thick, silvery-black bill.

Carrion Crow/Hooded Crow • *Corvus corone/cornix* 46cm, 18in

When Year round **Where** Farmland, hills, cliffs, moorland, woodland fringe. Carrion Crow, countrywide except some of Scotland and absent from Ireland, replaced there by Hooded Crow **Confusion species** Each other, Rooks, Jackdaw **Call** Harsh *kraa or caw*

▶ Hooded Crow is the northern form of Carrion Crow. Both have heavy black bills, round foreheads and flattish crowns, with square tails. Structurally identical, but Hooded instantly told by their grey and black plumage.

▶ In flight, note the square-ended tail and the bulge on the rear edge of the wing.

◀ **Hooded Crows** show black on the head, breast, wings and tail.The rest of the plumage is battleship grey, which, when the bird is seen in flight, presents a striking image. On a close view, note the fine black streaks on the underwing, upper breast, mantle and flanks.

▼ **Carrion Crow** is entirely black, with a hint of a purple gloss.The heftier, rounder bill,'shorts' rather than 'trousers' and a squarer tail separate them from Rooks.

▲ **Carrion Crows** are opportunistic feeders, with a well-balanced diet. Will happily eat fruit, grain, insects, worms, small mammals, bird's eggs, nestlings and carrion.

Rook • *Corvus frugilegus*

41-49cm, 16.5–19in

When Year round **Where** Breeds in open woodland, likes open farmland. Found everywhere, except northern Scotland **Confusion species** Carrion Crow, Raven, Jackdaw **Call** Distinctive *kaah*

Bulkier than Carrion Crows, with a pointed bill, pale face, high forehead and shaggy 'trousered' look about the legs.

◀ A familiar view of a rookery: dozens of birds nest in communal sites.

▼ **Adults** are glossy-black all over with a purple sheen. Base of bill, chin and lores show a large patch of whitish bare skin. Silvery bill with a dark tip.

▶ **Juveniles** resemble Carrion Crows. Plumage is dark brown, face is feathered. Bill darker than adults.

Raven • *Corvus corax*

54-67cm, 26in

When Throughout the year **Where** Uplands and coasts of western and northern England,Wales and Ireland. Incredibly rare elsewhere **Confusion species** Other corvids **Call** A far-carrying, rolling *krrronk*

Largest member of the Crow family (size of a Buzzard), but shy and wary.

▲ Notice the different shape of the **Raven** (far right) compared to the **Rook** (far left) and **Carrion Crow** (centre). Raven has a massive-looking head, long wings and characteristic wedge- shaped tail. Ravens are very acrobatic, tumbling and swooping in spectacular fashion.

▼ On the ground, note the very heavy bill, obvious shaggy throat feathers along with its size.

House Sparrow • *Passer domesticus*

14-16cm, 6.5in

When Year round **Where** Bushes, scrub, buildings and houses across Britain, breeding numbers falling **Confusion species** Tree Sparrow **Call** A simple *chatter* or *chirp*

One of our most familiar birds, but has recently seen a large decline in numbers.

▲ **Winter males** look rather dull. The crown and bib become pale and flecked white. Duller upperparts, yellowish bill.

▶ **Juveniles** resemble females, but are generally brighter, owing to their fresh new feathers.

◀ **Males** have a distinctive head pattern of grey, black, brown and white. Upperparts are brown, with darker streaking and the underparts have a grey wash. Note the black chin and breast, contrasting with white cheeks.

◀ **Females** have a broad creamy patch behind the eye, a tawny crown, black eyestripe, greyish cheeks and white chin. The wings show straw-yellow 'tramlines', bordered by black, golden-browns, charcoal-blacks and white.

Tree Sparrow • *Passer montanus*

12.5-14cm, 5.5in

When Year round. Spring and autumn passage **Where** Arable farmland, woodland fringe. Most of Britain, absent in south-west, Wales, much of Scotland and Ireland **Confusion species** House Sparrow **Call** A resonant, quick *tek-tek*

Smaller and neater than House Sparrow, but share a round head, shortish wings and plump body - and the plumage (for both sexes) is surprisingly bright.

▶ In flight, quicker and more agile than House Sparrow.

◀ **Juveniles** are a more subdued version of the adult. The head pattern is slightly different, with a greyish wash to the centre of the crown, merging into a less bright chestnut cap. Face pattern is less bright and the cheek spot less well defined.

▶ **Adults** have a chestnut cap, black bib and cheek patch, with a white neck collar. The mantle is warm-brown with bold streaks. The unmarked rump is yellow-buff, with a dark, notched tail. Note the double white wing bar. Underparts are white with light buff flanks. In winter, the bill shows a yellow base.

Chaffinch • *Fringilla coelebs*

14.5–16cm, 6in

When Year round, autumn/winter migrant **Where** Woodland fringe, farmland, parks and gardens across Britain **Confusion species** Brambling **Call** A soft *chip*

▶ In flight, bounding and undulating. White wingbars, greenish rump and white outer tail feathers.

◀ A slim, long-tailed sparrow-sized bird, massive influxes of continental birds can take place in the autumn. In winter, a **male's** head becomes grey and the underparts fade.

▶ **Males** have a blue-grey nape and crown, black forehead and russet cheeks. Pale lime-green rump fading to a grey central tail. Rest of tail is black with white outer feathers. Wings show a prominent white shoulder patch and wing bar.

◀ **Females** duller. Upperparts are generally fawn-brown, with darker head stripes and mantle. Rump patch is smaller and duller-green. Wing pattern as male, but duller.

Brambling • *Fringilla montifringilla* 14–15cm, 5.5in

When Arrives from September onwards, leaving in early spring **Where** Found in beech woodland and farmland across the country **Confusion species** Chaffinch **Call** A nasal *te-eup* (like squeaky hinge) also hard *yeck*

Similar in size and shape to Chaffinch. The two species are often seen together.

◀ **Non breeding males** have a grey nape. Orange shoulders and breast, thin white wingbars and white rump patch. Mantle is scalloped black on brown. Underparts fade from orange breast to white belly.

▶ **Females** have drabber head pattern. Orange on the wings and breast is more subdued.

▶ In flight, white rump patch is obvious. Note thin off-white wing- bars and orange shoulders.

Greenfinch • *Carduelis chloris* 14–15cm, 5.5in

When Year round **Where** Woodland around the country **Confusion species** None **Call** song delivered with butterfly display

A heavy bird with a stout head, body and bill. Frequently seen in gardens.

▶ In flight, note bright yellow tail flashes and forked black tail. Yellow on wing prominent.

▶ **Males** green, with areas of yellow, black and grey. Note paler yellow rump, and yellow tail sides. Wings show a strong yellow leading edge.

◀ **Females** are duller. Head is dark with paler supercilium and moustachials.

▲ **Juveniles** paler with streaked underparts. Yellow wing panel.

Serin • *Serinus serinus*

11–12cm, 4.5in

When Generally from late March to June, then August to October. Some wintering records. Rare, sporadic breeder **Where** Woodland, parkland, coastal bushes and weedy fields. Mainly southern Britain **Confusion species** Siskin, Greenfinch, escaped Canary **Call** Far-carrying song, a buzzy *ziir-irr-irr-irr,* clear and resonant

A tiny, rather dumpy-looking finch with a rather sweet-sounding jangling song. Has a yellow rump and an unmarked tail, wing pattern rather plain, plus a short stubby bill.

◀ Characteristic undulating flight. Yellow rump and double yellow wing bars obvious. Male has yellow collar, lacking on the greener female and streakier juvenile.

▶ A singing **male** Serin, bright yellow around face, extending onto the breast. Flanks show black streaks on white ground colour. Upperparts boldly streaked with black.

Siskin • *Carduelis spinus*

11.5–12.5cm, 4.5in

When Throughout the year **Where** Conifer plantations, alder and birch woods. Gardens in winter. Breeds East Anglia, south-west England, west coast of Ireland and Scotland. Countrywide in winter **Confusion species** Greenfinch, Serin **Call** A soft *telu or tl-leh*

Small, neat finches, with a smallish head and a short, forked tail.

▶ Forked tail and longish looking wings apparent in flight. Black and yellow on the male's upperwing is obvious.

▶ **Males** are strikingly green and yellow, with a black forehead and bib. Underparts show fine black streaks on white belly.

◀ **Females** are duller. Upperparts are * lime-green with fine dark streaks. Yellow on wings, paler than male.

◀ **Juveniles** have a distinctive breast and flank pattern.

Goldfinch • *Carduelis carduelis*

11.5-12.5cm, 5in

When Year round **Where** Scrub, cliff-top fringes, weedy fields, beaches, woodland and gardens. Countrywide (absent far north of Scotland) **Confusion species** None **Call** Clear, ringing *stickalit*. Song, a fast trilling twitter

A small, delicate finch, with a large pointed bill, rounded head, slim body and forked tail.

▲ In flight, the black and gold is obvious. Note the white rump, spots on the tail and two-toned underwing.

▲ Goldfinches are especially fond of thistle heads and are very agile as they remove seed heads. Large roving groups can be found along coasts in the winter, often joining other finches in big flocks.

▲ **Juveniles** have pale brown upperparts and a greyish head. Rump is buffish and the wings far duller. Underparts are buffish with dark streaks, particularly on the flanks.

▶ Both sexes similar. Distinctive face pattern, contrasting with rich-brown upperparts and flanks. The gold wing bar is very obvious; the rest of the wing is black with white tips. Black tail, with prominent white spots.

Linnet • *Carduelis cannabina*

13-14cm, 5.5in

When Year round **Where** Breeds from coasts to heaths, favouring gorse. Otherwise farmland, roadsides, rough ground countrywide **Confusion species** Twite, Common Rosefinch **Call** A dry *tigg-ett or teet-eet-eet*

▼**Females** (left) plain compared to male. Head streaked brown with greyish nape and creamy patches below the eye. Upperparts warm-brown, streaked blackish. Wings are strongly patterned black and white. Underparts show a buff-yellow wash on breast, streaked brown, fading to white.

▲Slim, relatively long-tailed birds, frequently seen in small family groups in late summer, larger flocks in winter.

◀**Breeding male.** (right) Deep pink forehead on grey and white head. Mantle is rich-russet and wings are marked strongly black, brown and white. Breast shows strong pinkish-red patches, fading to ochre on flanks. Rest of underparts are dull white.

Twite • *Carduelis flavirostris*

12.5-14cm, 5in

When Passage birds appear in autumn, many wintering **Where** Breeding birds in moorland areas of northern England, Scotland and Ireland. Passage birds mainly on east coast **Confusion species** Linnet, Lesser Redpoll **Call** Most frequently heard is a short, hard *cheet*

Similar in shape and size to Linnet, but has a longer-looking tail and rather different plumage.

◀Both sexes similar. Inconspicuous streaky-brown finches, pale throats, buffish flanks and indistinct wing bars. **Males** (right) show pink on the rump, and in autumn and winter, bill becomes yellowish.

Lesser Redpoll • *Carduelis cabaret* 12-13cm, 5in

When Year round. Migrants in winter **Where** Woodland, parkland and heaths throughout Britain **Confusion species** Common Redpoll **Call** A buzzing *jeet-jeet-jeet*

◀ **Females** show only a small amount of red on the cap and very little, if any, on breast. Rump tends to be browner.

◀ **Common Redpolls** (above and far right).

▶ **Males** (bottom) show a small red cap on the forehead, black lores and chin, with buff cheeks, and darker upperparts. Pale pink rump, dark brown wings with pale cream wingbars. White underparts show a pinky-red wash on the breast, flanks are streaked black.

Small, round little birds, with stubby bills, notched tails and gregarious habits. The various racial guises accounts for their erratic European distribution.

Common Redpoll • *Carduelis flammea* 12-15cm, 5.5in

When From late September through to March **Where** Mainly along northern and eastern coasts. Frequent inland in invasion years **Confusion species** Lesser Redpoll **Call** More nasal, buzzing and higher-pitched than Lesser, but still a *jeet-jeet-jeet*

Larger and paler than Lesser Redpoll. Bill size is variable, some looking 'squashed in' while others look long and broad.

▶ Originate from Scandinavia. Often referred to as Mealy Redpolls. Head and upperparts frosty grey-brown when compared to the warm brown of Lesser. **Adult males** are always the palest-looking birds. In late winter and early spring they show a beautiful rosy wash on the breast and rump.

▼ Both **female** (above) and male (right) have whiter-looking wing bars and rumps than Lesser. Underparts also look paler and whiter. Mantle much paler, looking hoar-frosted, and merges into pale-looking streaky rump.

Common Crossbill • *Loxia curvirostra*

15-17cm, 6-6.5in

When Throughout the year. Irruptions occur in late summer through to winter **Where** Breeds in conifer forests only in southern and northern England. Also in Scotland **Confusion species** Scottish Crossbill (Parrot Crossbill) **Call** Many calls, commonest being a strident *chip-chip*

◀ **Females** appear greyish-green all over with darker wings and yellowish rump. After breeding, some males can resemble females. Note the bill and notched tail. Juveniles are heavily-streaked all over, with a greenish tinge.

◀ **Males** unmistakable, burnt reddish-pink all over, except for darker wings and tail.

A fairly bulky-looking finch with very particular habitat preferences. Irruptions occur when pine crops are poor in Scandinavia.

Scottish Crossbill • *Loxia scotica*

15.5–17cm, 6–6.5in

When Year round **Where** Confined to pine forests of the Scottish Highlands **Confusion species** Common Crossbill (and the rarer Parrot Crossbill) **Call** Once thought to be a fail-safe identification point - a harder, less clipped *cheeup*

Currently the only endemic species in Britain. The identification and status of this bird are always being debated. In some areas of Scotland three Crossbill species are known to be breeding! Quite possibly the hardest (and least convincing) species to identify in Britain.

◀ Identical in every plumage respect to Common Crossbill but seem to have a slightly larger, broader-based bill.

Common Rosefinch • *Carpodacus erythrinus* 13.5-15cm, 6in

When Spring and autumn **Where** Bushes and weedy fields, often coastal. Spring birds tend to be in northern Britain, autumn more widespread **Confusion species** Linnet **Call** A repeated soft whistle - *vidyaa-vidyaa-vidyuuu* ('pleased to meet you')

Roughly the same size as a Greenfinch and although slimmer, looks more front-heavy. Largish bill, small head, slim rear end and long tail.

▶ **Breeding** males are stunning! Head and breast are crimson, with a brown eye patch. Upperparts are brownish, with crimson rump. The underparts show some faint streaking on the belly.

▼ More typical are **autumn juveniles** and **females** (below). They appear rather non-descript with faintly streaked green- brown upperparts, darker wings and contrasting double wingbars. Often the most striking feature of autumn birds are their teddy bear-like, black, beady eyes.

Bullfinch • *Pyrrhula pyrrhula*

14-15cm, 5.5–6in

When Throughout the year **Where** Scrubby hedgerows, orchards woodland and plantations across the country **Confusion species** None **Call** A soft, low-pitched *decaw*

▶ **Males** are strikingly black, grey and carmine-red. Head is glossy black.

▶ **Females** share the male's black cap and grey nape, but have a brownish-tinged mantle. White vent and undertail.

▲ In flight, the black cap, grey mantle of males, black and white wings, white rump patch and black tail are all distinguishing features.

▶ **Juveniles** have plain, brown heads.

Hawfinch • *Coccothraustes coccothraustes*

16–17cm, 6.5in

When Year round, best in winter **Where** Breeds in mixed and deciduous woods, especially with Hornbeam and Oak. Mainly England, Wales and southern Scotland **Confusion species** Chaffinch **Call** A metallic *zik-zik*

A large, sturdy bird, distinctive plumage, large triangular bill, large head and short tail.

▶ In flight, note the short, square tail, big head and bill. Broad white wing bar on inner wing and broad white tail band.

▲ **Males** have a russet-toned head, with black feathering around the bill base and chin. Lyre-shaped tertials seen with close view.

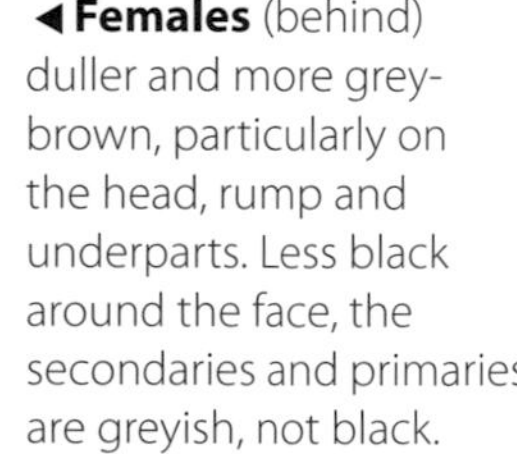

◀ **Females** (behind) duller and more grey-brown, particularly on the head, rump and underparts. Less black around the face, the secondaries and primaries are greyish, not black.

Corn Bunting • *Miliaria calandra*

16-19cm, 7-7.5in

When Throughout the year but a species that is, very much, in decline. Generally a fairly sedentary species but some individuals do move within the core range **Where** Breeds almost exclusively around areas of open arable farmland, mainly in southern and eastern England **Confusion species** None **Call** A short, metallic *kriitt*. Song distinctive, often likened to a bunch of jangling keys

▶ In flight, Corn Buntings generally looks pretty drab, appearing rather plain brown above, obviously off-white and pale below with a distinctive blackish 'necklace' on the breast, most obvious as a central spot. Note too the lack of white in the outer tail feathers (compared to a non-male Yellowhammer) and the dangling pale-yellowy legs.

This is a large, heavy-looking bunting, the largest you'll encounter, with rather nondescript plumage. In winter they are often found with other buntings, especially Yellowhammers and Reed Buntings.

▶ Sings from wires or fence posts, but hides in scrub too. Corn Buntings are generally streaky brown above, with an indistinct white rear supercilium and throat contrasting with darker areas on the ear coverts and remainder of the head. There are few defining marks to be seen on the upperparts, except for the striking row of covert feathers near the bend of the wing, white tipped and black centred. Underparts show many fine dark streaks on the whitish ground colour. Note again the heavy blob in the centre of the breast. Heavy straw-coloured bill and rather cute expression, thanks to beady black eyes.

Reed Bunting • *Emberiza schoeniclus*

14-15cm, 5.5in

When Year round **Where** Marshes, reedbeds, hedgerows, bushes and, particularly in winter, farmland. Found countrywide **Confusion species** Little Bunting **Call** Tinny, strident *tzeeo*

A medium-sized bunting with a rounded head, sometimes elongated body, and notched tail.

▼**Breeding males** have jet-black head, with a white moustachial stripe and collar. Upperparts are warm-chestnut, with bold mantle streaks and greyish, streaked rump.

▲**Non breeding females** have a greyer head than summer birds, with a yellowish wash on the supercilium and throat. More pronounced mark-ings on the breast and flanks.

▶**Breeding females** lack the males' black head. Crown and ear coverts dark, with a white supercilium. Underparts are white, except for the black malar.

Little Bunting • *Emberiza pusilla*

12-13.5cm, 5in

When Very rare, though annual, most frequent in autumn, some in winter and spring **Where** Scrub, weeds, crop fields, mainly coastal, wintering birds inland. Mainly north and east coasts **Confusion species** Reed Bunting **Call** A short, sharp *zik*

Little Buntings are exactly that - little! Structurally similar to Reed Bunting.

▼Striking head pattern, peaked crown striped black, reddish- brown median stripe (brighter on breeding birds).Face pale russet-brown, black ear covert, cream and black throat pattern. Note pale eye-ring, spot on ear coverts and silvery bill with straight culmen, unlike curved bill of Reed Bunting.

▶Upperparts cold-grey, with neat black streaking, finer on rump. Wings similar, grey with black feather centres, two narrow white wingbars. Underparts creamy white, with thin, narrow streaks on breast onto flanks.

◀Small birds, with distinctive plumage, bill shape and call.

▲**Breeding birds** brighter in plumage than non breeding birds, particularly around the face.

Lapland Bunting • *Calcarius lapponicus*

14-15.5cm, 6in

When Frequent in autumn and winter, very rare spring migrant **Where** Coastal fields, beaches, especially on east coast. Breeds in mountainous terrain in Scotland. Very rare breeding migrant **Confusion species** Sky Lark, Snow Bunting (on ground only) **Call** A dry sounding *prrrrrut*, harder sounding than Snow Bunting. Also a strident *tchu*

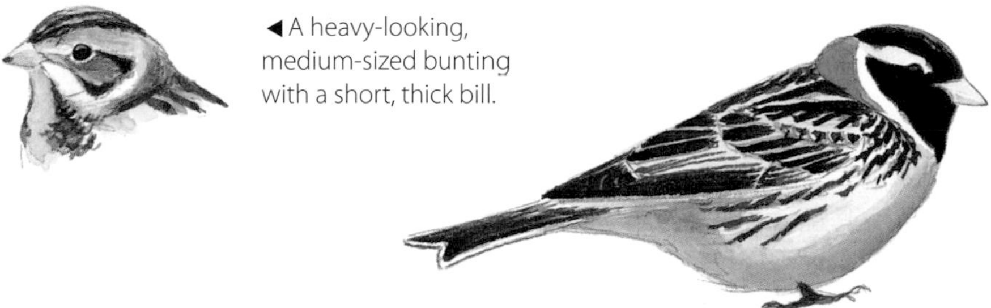

◄ A heavy-looking, medium-sized bunting with a short, thick bill.

▼ **Non breeding male** shows the double wingbars (and the ginger-brown greater coverts).They have a distinctive head pattern; a thin black line on the ear covert surround and dark, densely-streaked crown, the remainder of the face is warm-brown. Note the pronounced dark-spotted upper breast and malar stripe.

▲ **Breeding males** are unmistakable, with their striking black, white and rufous head pattern. Autumn birds are trickier - look for thin double white wingbars, a dark breast band and a brownish face with black ear covert surround.

Yellowhammer • *Emberiza citrinella* 16–17cm, 6.5in

When Year round. Absent from much of Ireland in winter **Where** Breeds in open farmland and hedgerows around the country **Confusion species** Cirl Bunting **Call** A metallic *zik* or *chip*. Song/A-little-bit-of-bread-no-cheese' of course!

Elongated birds with long wings and a longish notched tail. Recently numbers of breeding birds have dipped, primarily due to changes in agricultural methods.

▶ **Males** in flight show an obvious yellow head, dark wings, streaked mantle, plain rusty rump, long, dark tail and white outer feathers.

◀ **Juveniles** look like females, but have streakier heads, breasts and flanks (washed yellow) and are generally much duller.

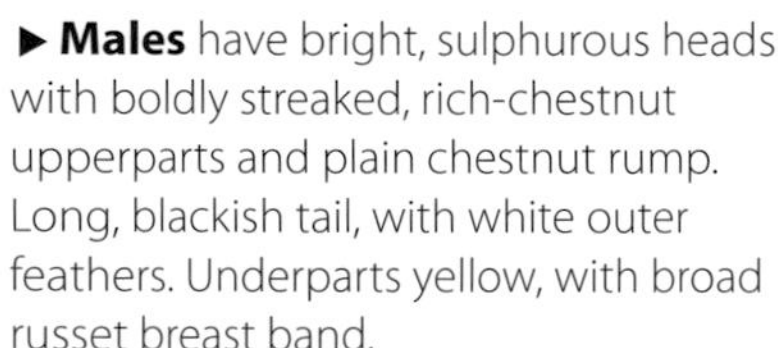

▶ **Males** have bright, sulphurous heads with boldly streaked, rich-chestnut upperparts and plain chestnut rump. Long, blackish tail, with white outer feathers. Underparts yellow, with broad russet breast band.

◀ **Females** share the male's unmarked rump and tail. Upperparts are streaky brown, with a yellow wash to the face. Yellowish underparts are streaked on breast and flanks.

Cirl Bunting • *Emberiza cirlus*

15-16.5cm, 6in

When Throughout the year, rare breeding species **Where** Trees, hedgerows and bushes on slopes. Southwest England only **Confusion species** Yellowhammer **Call** Sharp sounding *zit*. Song resonant, repeated *zree-zree-zree-zree*

Slightly smaller than Yellowhammer, with a larger bill and shorter tail.

▶ **Females** are like Yellowhammers, but have a streaked grey-brown rump, broader head stripes and a darker crown.

◀ **Males** are very handsome, with very striking, neat black and yellow face patterns, rich breast markings and warm-toned upperparts.

Ortolan Bunting • *Emberiza hortulana*

15-16.5cm, 6.5in

When Spring birds from late April to June, autumn birds from late August to October **Where** Coastal fields mainly, short turf ideally. Mainly along east and south coast **Confusion species** Other small buntings **Call** A metallic *slee-e, also pleeeet*

A medium-sized, fairly slim bird, with a longish bill and distinctive plumage.

Females have less colourful, slightly streaked heads, with duller underparts.

▼ **Juveniles** tend to be streakier. All have a yellow eye-ring and pinkish bill (with a dark culmen).

▲ **Spring males** have grey-green heads with yellow moustachials and throat. Upperparts brownish with darker streaks, the under parts are warm orangey-brown.

Snow Bunting • *Plectrophenax nivalis*

15.5-18cm, 7in

When Breeding birds appear mid-spring. Passage birds arrive from late September, leave by April **Where** Breeds on mountain tops of Scottish Highlands. Winters on north and east coast **Confusion species** Lapland Bunting, Sky Lark **Call** A single note *teew* or a jangling, drawn out twitter

▼ A **winter flock** of Snow Buntings will warm you, even on the bitterest of days. Flashes of white and black from winter males really do suggest a flurry of snow.

◀ Small- to medium-sized buntings, rarely seen in summer plumage here, but can be found on saltings, stubble fields on beaches in the winter.

▼ **Females** (left) are cute-looking birds, despite lacking the brighter plumage of males. Generally streaky-fawn-brown above and buff and white below, they appear rather dark on the upperwing.

▼ A **winter male** (right) gets progressively paler as the winter turns to spring. White face varies from bird to bird. Note the soft expression and, of course, the large white wing patches.

Tick list

- Mute Swan ☐
- Bewick's Swan ☐
- Taiga/Tundra Bean Goose ☐
- White-fronted Goose ☐
- Canada Goose ☐
- Brent Goose ☐
- Snow Goose ☐
- Shelduck ☐
- Ruddy Shelduck ☐
- Eurasian Wigeon ☐
- Gadwall ☐
- Common Teal ☐
- Mallard ☐
- Pintail ☐
- Shoveler ☐
- Red-crested Pochard ☐
- Ring-necked Duck ☐
- Tufted Duck ☐
- Greater Scaup ☐
- Common Eider ☐
- Long-tailed Duck ☐
- Surf Scoter ☐
- Red-breasted Merganser ☐
- Smew ☐
- Red Grouse ☐
- Black Grouse ☐
- Quail ☐
- Red-legged Partridge ☐
- Pheasant ☐
- Golden Pheasant ☐
- Red-throated Diver ☐
- Great Northern Diver ☐
- Great Crested Grebe ☐
- Red-necked Grebe ☐
- Slavonian Grebe ☐
- Gannet ☐
- Fulmar ☐
- Great Shearwater ☐
- Manx Shearwater ☐
- Storm-petrel ☐
- Great Cormorant ☐
- Shag ☐
- White Stork ☐
- Common Bittern ☐
- Grey Heron ☐
- Purple Heron ☐
- Red Kite ☐
- Honey Buzzard ☐
- Marsh Harrier ☐
- Hen Harrier ☐
- Sparrowhawk ☐
- Goshawk ☐
- Rough-legged Buzzard ☐
- Osprey ☐
- Golden Eagle ☐
- Merlin ☐
- Peregrine ☐
- Water Rail ☐
- Moorhen ☐
- Coot ☐
- Corncrake ☐
- Stone Curlew ☐
- Avocet ☐
- Lapwing ☐
- Grey Plover ☐
- Little Ringed Plover ☐
- Kentish Plover ☐
- Black-tailed Godwit ☐
- Whimbrel ☐
- Curlew ☐
- Ruff ☐
- Turnstone ☐
- Knot ☐
- Sanderling ☐
- Little Stint ☐
- Temminck's Stint ☐

Tick list (continued)

- Purple Sandpiper ☐
- Pectoral Sandpiper ☐
- Green Sandpiper ☐
- Common Redshank ☐
- Spotted Redshank ☐
- Woodcock ☐
- Common Snipe ☐
- Red-necked Phalarope ☐
- Pomarine Skua ☐
- Long-tailed Skua ☐
- Black Guillemot ☐
- Guillemot ☐
- Puffin ☐
- Black Tern ☐
- Common Tern ☐
- Arctic Tern ☐
- Little Tern ☐
- Kittiwake ☐
- Sabine's Gull ☐
- Little Gull ☐
- Great Black-backed Gull ☐
- Lesser Black-backed Gull ☐
- Herring Gull ☐
- Yellow-legged Gull ☐
- Iceland Gull ☐
- Common Gull ☐
- Rock Dove ☐
- Stock Dove ☐
- Collared Dove ☐
- Common Cuckoo ☐
- Ring-necked Parakeet ☐
- Little Owl ☐
- Short-eared Owl ☐
- Long-eared Owl ☐
- Common Swift ☐
- Common Kingfisher ☐
- Hoopoe ☐
- European Bee-eater ☐
- Green Woodpecker ☐
- Great Spotted Woodpecker ☐
- Lesser Spotted Woodpecker ☐
- Sky Lark ☐
- Wood Lark ☐
- Sand Martin ☐
- Swallow ☐
- House Martin ☐
- Yellow Wagtail ☐
- Grey Wagtail ☐
- Pied Wagtail ☐
- Richard's Pipit ☐
- Meadow Pipit ☐
- Tree Pipit ☐
- Rock Pipit ☐
- Waxwing ☐
- Dunnock ☐
- Wren ☐
- Robin ☐
- Bluethroat ☐
- Black Redstart ☐
- Whinchat ☐
- Ring Ouzel ☐
- Mistle Thrush ☐
- Fieldfare ☐
- Redwing ☐
- Lesser Whitethroat ☐
- Blackcap ☐
- Barred Warbler ☐
- Icterine Warbler ☐
- Sedge Warbler ☐
- Reed Warbler ☐
- Grasshopper Warbler ☐
- Goldcrest ☐
- Pallas's Warbler ☐
- Wood Warbler ☐
- Chiffchaff ☐
- Willow Warbler ☐
- Spotted Flycatcher ☐
- Pied Flycatcher ☐

Tick list (continued)

- Blue Tit ☐
- Crested TitMarsh Tit ☐
- Willow Tit ☐
- Long-tailed Tit ☐
- Bearded Tit ☐
- Nuthatch ☐
- Common Treecreeper ☐
- Golden Oriole ☐
- Red-backed Shrike ☐
- Starling ☐
- Chough ☐
- Magpie ☐
- Jay ☐
- Carrion Crow/Hooded Crow ☐
- Rook ☐
- House Sparrow ☐
- Tree Sparrow ☐
- Chaffinch ☐
- Brambling ☐
- Serin ☐
- Goldfinch ☐
- Linnet ☐
- Lesser Redpoll ☐
- Common Crossbill ☐
- Common Rosefinch ☐
- Bullfinch ☐
- Corn Bunting ☐
- Reed Bunting ☐
- Lapland Bunting ☐
- Yellowhammer ☐
- Cirl Bunting ☐
- Snow Bunting ☐

Glossary

Bird of prey member of the large group of species that hunt and feed on other birds or animals – includes hawks, falcons, harriers, buzzards

Call different from song! Calls can be many and varied – used as a contact between individuals, a warning of danger or a declaration of territory

Feral birds that sustain a wild population from introduced or escaped stock

Irruption occurs in winter when large groups of one species arrive from Europe. Dependent on food shortages in European wintering grounds

Juvenile bird of that year, which fledges successfully from chick stage

Lek ritualistic display, in which many males of a species parade at a female

Non-passerine any species that does not fall into the Passerine group

Passage movement through an area, of birds that neither breed nor spend the winter there, merely passing through on migration

Passerine member of the large group Passeriformes, called 'perching birds' (literally 'sparrow-like' birds)

Raptor member of the order Falconifores, which contains the diurnal birds of prey

Song complex series of sounds produced by a (usually male) bird for the purposes of attracting a mate and/or defending a territory against others of its species

Taxonomy description of the external features of a bird

Vagrant bird that wanders to an area if its orientation is at fault or adverse winds drive it off course but would not normally be found there

Wader species that is reliant on feeding and breeding in wetland habitats

Winter/Over-winter bird that visits an area for the winter only and does not breed there. Birds that 'over-winter' are summer migrants that then choose not to migrate

Acknowledgements

Firstly, I would like to thank Jane Lawes, the Natural History Editor at Bloomsbury, for her help in bringing this project together safely and in one piece. I would also like to acknowledge the skill of artist Dave Daly, he does bring a certain something to the birds featured within.

Finally, thanks to Nadine and our trusty tabby Ted.

Further reading

Blake, Nigel, *Bloomsbury Pocket Guide to Garden Birds*, Bloomsbury, 2014

Brooke, Michael and Birkhead, Tim, *Cambridge Encyclopedia of Ornithology,* Cambridge University Press, 1991

Golley, Mark, *The Complete Garden Bird Book*, New Holland Publishers, 2001

Hammond, Nicholas (Series Editor), *The Wildlife Trusts Guide to Birds*, New Holland Publishers, 2002

Hammond Nicholas, *The Wildlife Trusts Handbook of Garden Wildlife,* Bloomsbury, 2014

Holden, Peter and Cleeves, Tim, *RSPB Handbook of British Birds*, *4th edition,* Bloomsbury, 2014

Moss, Stephen, *The Garden Bird Handbook*, New Holland Publishers, 2003

Moss, Stephen, *Understanding Bird Behaviour,* Bloomsbury, 2015

Oddie, Bill, *Bill Oddie's Birds of Britain and Ireland*, New Holland, 2001

Tipling, David, *Top Birding Spots in Britain and Ireland*, HarperCollins, 1996

Useful websites

The Wildlife Trusts
www.wildlifetrusts.org

Wildlife Watch
www.wildlifewatch.org.uk

Birding World magazine
www.birdingworld.co.uk

Birdwatch magazine
www.birdwatch.co.uk

Bird Watching magazine
www.birdwatching.co.uk

British Birds magazine
www.britishbirds.co.uk

British Trust for Ornithology (BTO)
www.bto.org

Royal Society for the Protection of Birds (RSPB)
www.rspb.org.uk

Subbuteo Natural History Books Ltd
www.wildlifebooks.com

Wildfowl and Wetlands Trust
www.wwt.org.uk

Wildsounds
www.wildsounds.com

Index

Index (continued)

Index (continued)